The Decoupage Workshop

Books by Leslie Linsley

THE DECOUPAGE WORKSHOP

SCRIMSHAW

DECOUPAGE DESIGNS

DECOUPAGE, A NEW LOOK AT AN OLD CRAFT

The Decoupage Workshop

by Leslie Linsley

Photography by Jon Aron

Doubleday & Company, Inc., Garden City, New York   1976

ACKNOWLEDGMENTS:

To be able to write a craft book with someone taking photographs every time you feel like working is probably a craftsperson's dream. I could never have done this book without Jon Aron.
Thanks also to Phil Rose for assuring quality control on the
black-and-white prints and to Karen Van Westering, a fine editor.

Library of Congress Cataloging in Publication Data

Linsley, Leslie.
  The decoupage workshop.

  SUMMARY: A detailed explanation of the decoupage
process with suggestions for projects and designs.
    1. Decoupage. [1. Decoupage. 2. Handicraft]
I. Aron, Jon. II. Title.
TT870.L542   745.54
ISBN: 0-385-07702-5
Library of Congress Catalog Card Number 76–2790

Contents

Decoupage, what is it? 15

   A first project 21
   What could be more basic than a radish? 22

Buying supplies: what, where, how much 26

   Paint 28
   Stain versus paint 28
   Sandpaper 30
   Item to be decoupaged 30
   Brush 32
   Varnish 32
   Shellac isn't varnish 33
   Brush cleaner 35
   Antiquing mix 36
   Where to find decoupage prints 36
   There is no substitute for cuticle scissors 40
   Using a tack cloth 41
   Wax 42

Decoupage processes: learning by doing 44

   If you don't like radishes 44
   One summer in Nantucket 45
   Applying paint 50
   Decoupage designs 53
   Cutting 55
   Arranging prints 58
   Gluing: after this there's no undoing 60
   What makes a superb finish 68
   Antiquing: you're not getting older, just better 71

What you cut is what you get   74

   A delicate piece   74
   Cutting tiny things   84

New ideas for outdoor projects   85

   Address oval   85
   Judy and Joel's jeep   90
   Decoupage on the high seas   98

Inspiration for designs   102

   What am I bid for this box of junk?   102
   What's your style?   104
   Design subtleties   107

Decoupage on furniture   110

   An undressed dresser   112
   Posters for design   114
   My apologies to Henri Rousseau   124
   A director's chair or two   137

Decoupage on metal   141

   Yes you can   143
   How to decoupage a trunk for under $5.00   144
   A doll's trunk   148

Boxes   149

   Where to find them   149
   How to make gramp's boxes   153
   Making a box with a half-round or elliptical lid   155
   A slip-on cover   155
   Designing a box   158
   Lining a box with paper   167
   Lining a box with fabric   168

Unusual projects   170

    Decoupage a lamp shade   170
    A three-paneled screen   170
    Decoupage on ceramic   172
    Decoupage under glass   174
    Photographs   176
    Photo collage (a family portrait)   178
    Christmas ornaments   180
    But not the kitchen sink   183
    A wallpaper project   184

Teaching decoupage   187

There is no end   192

AUTHOR'S NOTE:

Since all of you who are interested in decoupage can't come to my studio workshop, I have written this book as if you were there. I've tried to anticipate the questions you might ask and to select a variety of projects that will illustrate the many different techniques of the craft. The projects are ones that I chose to work on because they mean something to me. They represent my personal approach to the craft.

At root, I am a trial-and-error craft designer. When working with decoupage I often feel it is better to jump in and try new projects, even if they don't turn out the way I expected, rather than to advance cautiously. So this book is written from one craftsworker's point of view with the idea of sharing my experiences, both good and bad, in order that you might learn the hows and whys of designing as well as specific ideas for your own projects. I hope to open up the possibility for creative expression in each of you. So come into my workshop, and let's begin.

L.L.

PHOTOGRAPHER'S NOTE:

I find it fascinating to see a craft project develop, and I have photographed Leslie doing hundreds of projects. Often she chooses something to decoupage that is so miserable looking that I can't imagine what potential she sees in it. But, inevitably, she works with it until something quite beautiful emerges. On completion of a project I review the photographs taken along the way. The steps have been recorded accurately. Yet there is an ingredient that always eludes the eye of the camera.

You can see the results of the creative process, but you can't see the process itself . . . and, therefore, you can't take a picture of it.

The pictures in this book represent the visible results of that process.

JON ARON

The Decoupage Workshop

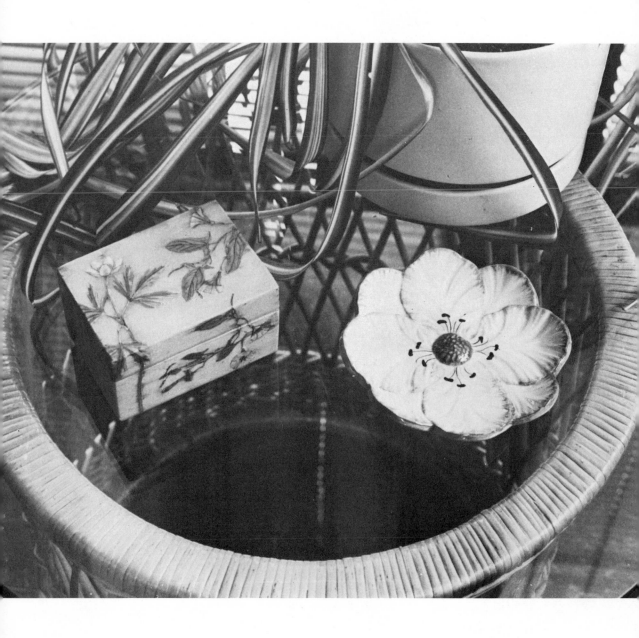

Decoupage: what is it?

There's a decoupaged box on the coffee table. There's another in the book case and another on a shelf. The silverware is housed in a chest decoupaged with oriental designs. A lap desk holds pens and papers on the piano. Decoupage candlesticks and napkin rings sit on the dining room table, and there are four different decoupaged egg cups in the kitchen. A flower pot with decoupaged leaves holds a hanging plant, and outside is a sign that welcomes you with number "78" decoupaged on an address oval. And there is more. "When do you turn a hobby into a business?" I'm often asked. I guess it's when you are forced to ask yourself, "Do they go, or do I go?"

Decoupage, the eighteenth-century craft that originated in France and Italy has emerged as the most popular craft of the 1970s. And why not? It's fairly easy to do, can be done in a small space, costs very little, and the materials are readily available. Further, a person can be creative with decoupage without any art training, and anyone can do it from children to old people. When you see the beautiful professional results that can be achieved, it is easy to understand why this craft has become so popular.

Decoupage is a craft that has been practiced in almost every country in the world, and the best part about it is that you can start it right now. Decoupage does require a bit of patience, but if you supply the patience, I'll supply the necessary instructions to make it a breeze.

The process of decoupage is to paint and decorate objects of wood or metal with cutout paper designs. Historically, it was "the poor man's art," but I prefer to describe decoupage as the craft of creating designs on a three-dimensional object with the simple tools of scissors, paper, and glue. Decoupage allows you the freedom to be as creative as you feel, and because of this freedom some very elaborate decoupage designs have emerged over the years.

Influenced by the very formal lacquered Japanese furniture, people originally applied decoupage to furniture. Today, decoupage is found mostly on small items such as boxes or wall plaques. Perhaps this is because we are living in a faster-paced society, and while the trend has shifted to handmade items, we are still not quite ready to spend months working on a single project. Years ago it literally could take six months to complete a decoupage piece, but today it is possible to finish a small project in just a few hours. There are new products on the market that produce beautiful effects without the tedious waiting and working of years ago.

Quickly, the decoupage process goes like this: First the object is sanded until it is smooth. Then it is painted with either a water-base or oil paint, depending on the object and its use. After the paint dries, it must be sanded lightly to remove any bumps or particles caused by the paint. Another coat of paint is applied, allowed to dry, and sanded again. Sometimes a third coat of paint is required. When using water-base paint this process doesn't take long because the paint dries quickly. Fine cuticle scissors are used to cut out designs from a print, a book, or similar source. Using a white glue, such as Elmer's Glue-All, the design is applied to the object where it looks best. Once it is securely in place a thin coat of varnish is applied to the entire object. The varnish coating takes twenty-four hours to dry if it is an oil base, fifteen minutes if it is a water base. When the varnish is dry another coat is applied. After three or four coats of varnish have been applied to the object, it is ready to be sanded. Use a super-fine sandpaper, such as 3M "Wetordry," sand very lightly over the entire surface, print and all. This must be done lightly so that the design won't be rubbed off. More coats of varnish are brushed on, and each is sanded after it is completely dry. When there are sufficient coats of varnish on the box—so that you can no longer lift up a corner of the design—an antique finish may be applied if desired. After this, a final coat of varnish is brushed over the entire object, and when it is dry a coat of wax is applied to preserve it forever.

For the beginner who is venturing forth on this new activity it can be pretty confusing. There are all kinds of quick-and-easy decoupage products. There is one-coat decoupage, transfer decal prints, fancy names that sound like decoupage, and many different kinds of finishes. What is real decoupage? And what is the difference between a one-coat finish and a piece that takes a week to coat with varnish? To answer that, let's look at painting. You can learn to paint a picture in all kinds of ways. If you really want to master the art of drawing and painting, then it is best to get instruction from an expert through a class or a book. You would learn not only the technical skills of painting and drawing, but also which materials to use and how best to use them. You also might experiment with different paints, brushes, etc. in order to achieve various results. On the other hand, if you just want to reap the rewards of a finished painting, you can buy a paint-by-numbers activity kit. It might be fun to do a project this way, but you wouldn't really learn how to paint even though the end results might be quite good.

Decoupage is the art of cutting out and applying paper designs. If you use a rub-on transfer design, you have eliminated one of the basic skills of decoupage. You have also limited the possibilities of creating your own designed piece, as you can't arrange it the way you want. The amount of varnish that you apply to your cutout print (which is slightly raised from the surface you are working on) affects the look or feel of the piece. With one-coat decoupage, which is actually a plastic resin that is poured on, this variety is lost. It is similar to embedding your design in plastic as you might do if you are making a paperweight. This is terrific for a quick project, but it is by no means decoupage.

The craft of decoupage is a total experience. It is not merely the finished result. As you work on a piece and watch it change from a simple crude piece of wood into an elegant handcrafted object, you are putting a bit of yourself into that work. The more you work on it, the more in tune with yourself you will feel. It is a very exciting and fulfilling experience that can't be achieved without going through each process. The feel of the wood as you sand it smooth, the brushing on of each coat of varnish and the gradual luster that begins to emerge after each new coat is applied are all a part of the craft. There is a relationship between the craftsworker and the object being crafted that simply is not present in "instant" decoupage. Of course, there are always short cuts to be learned as new materials are developed to replace the old. But that is not the same thing. For instance, as little as forty years ago varnish was a relatively new product, and shellac was the accepted finish for furniture. Today we know that varnish is a much harder and finer

finish, although shellac is still widely used. Polyurethane is a relatively new material and for some uses much better than varnish. There are also water-base finishes that dry in minutes as opposed to varnish that takes twenty-four hours to dry. The finish is not as fine or impervious to damage, but it is a marvelous new material for many purposes. All of these new products and others provide useful alternatives that expand the creative possibilities of decoupage, rather than limit it. In this jet age there is "instant" whatever you want, but if you want to learn the art and craft of decoupage, you must take the long rather than short cut.

A trinket box is a good first project.

A first project

A first project should be one that is small and can be finished quickly. When I teach children I find they are often impatient and can't be bothered finishing the job. They just want to get the pictures glued down and "don't tell me how to do it, thank you," and they're finished. But if you are really serious about learning this craft, it's important to do all the steps, even the first time. Select a small item such as a trinket box, or a plaque, because you will be able to design it easily and make fewer mistakes. You will become familiar with the materials and in a short period of time, without much expense, you will have gotten your feet wet. All the materials you need are available in local craft shops—and some you may even have at home.

A box is a good project to start with because it will enable you to design on a three-dimensional object. However, most people begin their decoupage experience with a plaque. This is the simplest because you are working only with one side—a flat surface. I must admit that I don't really care for plaque projects because they involve so little imagination. However, if you are a bit timid about decoupage, do start with a plaque. But give it some thought and come up with something that is beautifully designed no matter how simple.

To begin, we will go through a project together in order for you to become familiar with what's involved. I realize that you want to know where to get supplies and where to find good sources for prints, but before you run out to buy everything let me show you how it's done.

What could be more basic than a radish?

Sanding

Painting

Perhaps you've turned to this chapter because you read it in the table of contents and wonder how radishes can possibly relate to decoupage.

One day about a year ago Jon Aron received a promotional booklet from Warren Paper Company. It was a delightful book showing different artists' interpretations of a simple radish. We were working on this book together at the time, and he gave me the booklet which I saved, thinking I would do something with those illustrations. In order to illustrate how easy it is to create beautiful results with decoupage, I thought it might be fun to start with a beautiful, simple object and I remembered that booklet of radishes. Actually, there is nothing terribly beautiful about a radish, and as one artist put it, the radish is a rather puny-looking vegetable. But I think you'll agree that the illustration used here is quite elegant, a tribute to the artist, not the radish.

In this case we will be using a plaque, so choosing the right size board for the subject is the first consideration. The only way to decide this is to hold the print up to different

Cutting

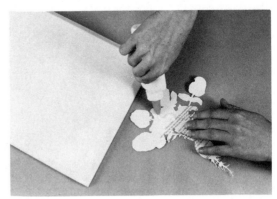

Gluing

sized plaques to see on which it will look best. If you plan to have a plaque made, you might first try drawing different sizes on a piece of paper until you like the results. Measure it and have the plaque made to that size.

The wood plaque can be either stained with a wood stain or painted with a color contrasting with the print. The first thing to do is sand the plaque smooth so that you have an even surface to work on. When your surface is smoothly sanded, wipe off the dust and apply one coat of paint. When this dries another coat of paint will be needed. Here I used white paint for the background and this color often requires a third coat of paint. If you are using a darker color, two coats is usually sufficient. Sand the last coat of paint lightly to regain your smooth surface. The wetness of the paint raises the grain of the wood. Using a fine cuticle scissors cut out the design. I used only the large radish and eliminated the other drawings in the print. Decide where you will place your design and then coat the back of the print with glue, spreading the glue to all edges. Lay the print in place. In this case, I centered the

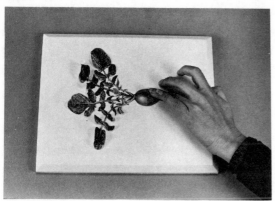

Placing Design   *Varnishing*

radish. Remember, once it is glued down it cannot be removed successfully.

Press the design down lightly with the palm of your hand and then, using a slightly damp sponge, pat away all excess glue that oozes out of the edges. The glue will dry in a few moments. Next, a varnish finish is brushed over the entire plaque, and it is set aside to dry. When the varnish is completely dry (usually in twenty-four hours) apply another coat of varnish. When there are three coats of varnish on your plaque it should be sanded lightly. More coats of varnish are applied and each is allowed to dry thoroughly before it is sanded smooth. When you feel there are sufficient coatings of varnish the piece is ready to be antiqued. How many coats are sufficient? When your piece has approximately ten coats of varnish your design will be submerged so that your design and plaque are smooth to the touch. I like the "sculptured effect" of a design slightly raised rather than submerged completely under the varnish, but this is up to you. The more coats of varnish you apply, the less raised your design will be. Antiquing is an optional step, but one I

Antiquing

always include because, if handled properly, it adds another dimension to the work. The antiquing mix is brushed on and then wiped off, leaving traces here and there for accent. When this dries another coat of varnish is put on to protect the antiquing. The work is once again set aside to dry. Then it is lightly sanded and protected with furniture paste wax, which, when buffed, gives your plaque the beautiful shine found only on fine furniture pieces.

There is, of course, a little more to decoupage than this, and that is where the fun and craftsmanship come in. The more you do this craft, the more knowledgeable you become. You will begin to look for things to decoupage and designs that you can create. You will strive for a better finish with each new project. You will probably run into little problems, but you will learn to solve them, and you will begin to realize a satisfaction that is gained from perfecting a new skill.

Buying supplies:
what, where, how much

The more you do decoupage, the more familiar you will become with your materials. Before long you will know which products you like better than others and which things work best for you. But before you are able to decide for yourself you will need the basic tools of the trade to start.

All the materials used in decoupage are quite familiar and there is nothing on the list that is difficult to get. Hardware stores used to be the only place to find these supplies. This often presented a problem since the hardware store owner didn't know what in the world decoupage was and, therefore, couldn't provide much help to the beginner. However, craft shops are now found in almost every town, and decoupage has become so popular that the owner is usually quite knowledgeable about the craft and its supplies. (Whenever possible, I advocate using what you have already bought for other uses, but a well-supplied craft shop is a great place to visit.)

These stores can be pretty confusing, however, if you don't have a basic list of supplies to start with. As I mentioned before, all the fancy names and products can be too much to cope with until you have had some experience yourself. So for the first project I recommend sticking with the basics. You can move on to experimentation when you feel more comfortable with the craft.

This is the basic list you will need for a first project:

1. Item to be decoupaged (this is entirely up to you, but keep it small)

2. Decoupage print (if you haven't got something that you have been saving to use for decoupage)

3. Cuticle scissors

4. Sandpaper (fine and medium grit)

5. Paint (water base is best the first time around)

6. Brush (choose the size appropriate to the object)

7. Varnish (don't fall apart, read further for different kinds)

8. Brush cleaner

9. Antiquing mix (this is optional)

10. Wax (furniture paste wax)

11. Tack cloth (or a clean rag is fine)

When you buy materials you should be sure you are getting the best-quality supplies for your money. Spend some time deciding and don't buy more than you'll need. Part of the appeal of this craft is that it doesn't cost much to get started. On the other hand, you will be putting a lot of your time and creative efforts into the project, so that the materials you use should be worthy of it and able to produce good results. For instance, you might be tempted to use a cigar box to see if you like decoupage and if you can make a nice looking box. Well, in my opinion this isn't the way to go about it. If you were learning to sew and decided to use the cheapest material you could find to make a dress, no matter how well made the dress was you probably wouldn't want to wear it. Using a cigar box is the same thing. You aren't giving decoupage a fair chance. Also, if you start out with a nice wood object you will probably take more time and care with the project, and it is bound to turn out better.

Paint

What kind of paint should you use? There are many different kinds of paint used for decoupage, but the most common is acrylic paint. This is available in a wide variety of colors, in jars and in tubes, and you can buy it in small quantities. It is thinned with water, your brush is cleaned with water, and it is easy to use. Acrylic paint gives your piece a beautiful finish and covers your item in one or two coats.

Oil-base paint, such as enamel, is thinned with turpentine or mineral spirits. This type of paint is a bit harder to use and is usually not carried in craft shops. However, you should use a good oil-base paint for any furniture project. Once dry it will not chip or peel and will last forever. It must be applied with more care since once dry it is more difficult to sand smooth than the acrylic or latex paint. Latex wall paint is excellent for decoupage. Most people have some in the house, and it is easy to use. Unlike the oil-base paint it dries quickly and can be cleaned up with water. It usually requires more coats to cover a piece, but they dry within fifteen minutes. It sands smooth easily and can be mixed in a variety of colors by your paint store or yourself. For small projects, use a tube of water-base acrylic paint in the color of your choice. This is excellent for decoupage but expensive in large quantities.

A dull surface is much more desirable than a glossy or semi-gloss finish for decoupage. Paint should not be too thick, and it should level out when it is applied or you will have an uneven surface that must be sanded until smooth enough to apply your designs.

Stain
versus paint

You may wonder whether to paint or stain a box or plaque, etc., for decoupage. How do you decide? Stains are generally used to bring out the beauty of the grain of wood or to emphasize the color. Most wood items sold for decoupage use are not made of the finest wood. This is understandable since they are most often painted and completely covered. However, if you have made or found an item of such lovely wood that it seems criminal to cover it— don't! When working on my first book, I came across a delightful candlestick made of a wood that had a beautiful swirling grain. I'm not sure of the kind of wood, but it had been painted and then later stripped. I did not repaint this piece, but rather designed it with a lacy pattern that blended with the natural beauty of the wood. The varnish finish then gave it an added dimension. Although I left it as is, this wood candlestick could also have been stained.

Woods such as cherry, walnut, and sometimes pine, have a natural color and pattern that is often too beautiful to cover. When the varnish finish is applied it darkens the wood somewhat and brings out the natural grain. Stain is different from a finish and will add color to wood that has no pretty natural color or beauty. I generally use an oil wood stain such as Minwax which is available in many wood colors at most hardware stores.

It is not difficult to stain and takes less time than painting, but before choosing the color stain pick out the designs you will use so that you can be sure they will show up against the background stain. While the stain is easy to apply, it must dry overnight before the decoupage process can proceed.

Subtle design applied to bare wood.

Sandpaper

The sandpaper that I like best is 3M "Wetordry." A medium-grade grit is used for the first sanding in order to smooth your wood for painting. After that you use a very fine black grit for sanding between coats of varnish. All abrasive papers come in various grades of fine or coarse grits and are marked accordingly on the back of each sheet. They are available in hardware stores. The medium-grade papers are usually referred to as cabinet papers, the fine grit as finishing papers, and the waterproof papers, such as 3M "Wetordry" sandpaper, are used for polishing to a fine finish. The latter are usually black and are best for the final sanding. Craft shops also sell prepackaged sandpaper for decoupage.

If you are planning to do a piece of furniture and will be using an electric sander, you should buy a different type of sandpaper. These also come in packages of different "weight" for sanding discs. Packaged strips for a sanding block are also available. These are usually found only in hardware stores, not craft shops.

Item to be decoupaged

Boxes or plaques are usually available in a variety of sizes at local craft shops. However, many of you might already have an old wooden recipe box or jewelry box that you'd like to redo with decoupage. Antique shops, thrift shops, attics, and tag sales are inexpensive ways of finding unusual items to decoupage. If you are handy with tools, you might want to try making your own boxes. Decoupage can also be done on metal, ceramic, under glass, and sometimes even on plastic (although this is the least desirable). You might have something tucked away that you can use, or you might just stumble over something that is just right—the way I did with the candlestick.

Often Jon and I go hunting for things. That's pretty general I know, but that's really what we do. We hop in the car and just take off. We are never sure what we're after or exactly where we're going. We only know that we have a general direction, and we will almost certainly find something to decoupage or at least write about. You know "the fish that got away" story. Well sometimes that's us—the

fabulous piece that we almost bought, but it was too big to fit in the car, or too expensive, or not just right. But we always see things that spark ideas.

On one particular jaunt we came across old crocks. Lots and lots of them. When there is a lot of something sitting right there somehow it's more impressive than just one of that something. With one you might look at it, pick it up, mull over the $2.00 price tag, go on to other things, and maybe come back to it. When there are fifty of something you tend to say, "That could be decoupaged." Then you walk away only to see more. Anyway I tucked one under my arm and decided it might do for a flower holder or for wooden spoons in the kitchen. I still haven't made anything of it, but often things have to sit until an idea or a really great design gels.

Clay pots can be decoupaged for plant holders.

Brush

I often recommend that a beginner buy an inexpensive, but good brush and use it for their entire project. This means that the same brush can be used for painting as well as varnishing provided it is kept clean. This is fine for a one-time use. However, if you are planning to go on and do more projects, it is a good idea to have two brushes—one for painting and one for varnishing. For most decoupage projects, the largest brush I use is a one-inch brush. For boxes and smaller items, a half-inch brush is better. It is difficult to use a larger brush on small items, and the painting probably will be downright messy. I don't believe in removing hinges. Therefore I have to be a bit more careful when painting, and for this I find a small brush is best. A quarter-inch brush is the best size for antiquing because you can get into little corners, around hinges, etc.

A natural-hair brush that costs under a dollar is great for painting and varnishing. It is a flat brush, usually referred to as a varnish brush. When using this kind of brush you should pull out the loose bristles so that they won't shed on your wet surface. This can be troublesome, and when it happens the only thing to do is to pick the hair off your piece. If it has dried there, it should be sanded off or removed with a razor blade.

A polyfoam brush is an inexpensive brush that looks like a piece of foam rubber on the end of a stick. They usually sell from thirty to fifty cents and are terrific for one-time use. After the job is over you throw it away because it will probably harden or flake apart. It does provide an even finish with no brush strokes to sand down. Because it is a sponge, however, it soaks up the material and your paint or varnish will not go as far as with a bristle brush.

For the best finish, be sure the brush is absolutely clean. While you can use any old brush for applying a paint remover, a new clean brush is the guaranteed way to apply a new finish. So if you were planning to save the dollar and use an old brush, forget it. It's not worth it. Spend the dollar and do it right.

Varnish

I don't know why it is, but everyone seems to fall apart at the idea of selecting a varnish. Or maybe it's not the selecting part. Maybe it's the doing. At any rate, before you do it you have to buy it. And before you buy it you have to know what you're buying.

This is one area that can be most confusing to a beginner when confronted with the various brands that fill the craft shop shelves. If you are buying supplies at the hardware store, it is even more baffling. At least in the craft shop the finishes say "for decoupage," not that that's much of a help when you are trying to decide whether you want a dull antique look or a glossy one.

There are all kinds of varnish finishes for decoupage, and the only kind NOT to use is spar varnish, unless you are decoupaging a boat (which, as a matter of fact, I did). The most common finishes are a satin or matte finish or a glossy finish. They both come in indoor wood varnish. When buying varnish it is best to buy it in small quantities. Varnish spoils when exposed to air and begins to form a hard surface or "skin" once opened. If this happens, and it takes weeks, just poke a hole in the top and lift it off with your brush handle. However, since it does not last forever it is best to buy varnish as you need it.

Shellac isn't
varnish

I often hear people refer to varnish as shellac, and I find that most people either don't know the difference or think they are one and the same. Pure shellac has one major advantage over pure varnish—it dries quickly. Almost all furniture has a shellac finish even though we are often told that it has a fine varnished finish. This is because the only way to apply a good coat of varnish is by hand, while shellac is almost always sprayed on. It goes on in a very thin coat and dries in fifteen minutes. Another advantage of shellac for furniture makers is that once thinned it does not create the air bubbles that often plague varnish users.

But in decoupage we never use shellac, only varnish, for several reasons. The biggest disadvantage of shellac is that it can be dissolved in alcohol. If you spill an alcoholic drink on a shellacked counter top, for instance, it will immediately dissolve the finish. If you have shellacked a coffee table and someone places a glass on it, the water ring will remain white as well as any water spots that may have dropped. If you use shellac on a decoupaged purse and go out in the rain or spill something on it, its finish will be marred. Therefore, I never use shellac as a finish. On the other hand, if you are applying your decoupage right onto bare wood, assuming it has first been sanded smooth, you can use shellac as a sealer. It is excellent for this use because it dries quickly and then you can apply your many coats of varnish right over it. This helps subsequent coats of varnish to dry more quickly.

Varnish is a synthetic resin that can be thinned with turpentine, paint thinner, or mineral spirits. It forms a very hard surface when it has been allowed to dry thoroughly, and the only way to remove it is with paint remover and lots of scraping and sanding. Nothing will mar the finish and you can spill anything on it without it being harmed. I usually use the varnish right out of the can, but once I have opened it a few times and it is no longer fresh, I thin it slightly with turpentine or mineral spirits. For the best results, your piece should be absolutely clean and free of sand, grit, or dust. There is nothing like a brand new can of varnish combined with a clean brush to insure a perfect decoupage finish.

Assuming that I've convinced you that the only route to go is varnish, the next question you should be asking is, "What kind?" As mentioned earlier, there are two kinds of finishes, one very different from the other. There is a very glossy finish and a matte or satin finish. Actually, the varnish that produces a glossy finish creates a harder surface, but the effect is nothing to compare with the satin or velvety finish. This is soft and mellow and gives the effect similar to a fine furniture patina. If the varnish finish is allowed to dry for a full twenty-four hours, you will have a really beautiful hard surface. The drying time is crucial. If you apply a coat of varnish and don't let it dry completely, what you are creating is a soft build-up that will eventually peel right off.

There are a few problems that arise when varnishing, but it isn't difficult at all. I guess varnishing is best learned by doing rather than reading about. One of the problems is air bubbles. Little bumps caused by air in the varnish often appear on the surface of your object. These can be eliminated by careful sanding when the varnish dries. Later on, when you are doing some projects, we'll discuss what the real problems are (there aren't many) and how to avoid them.

A lot of chemicals are labeled "brush cleaner," and it might be a good idea to know what they are and what else you can do with them besides clean your brush. Usually brush cleaner is used to clean your brush after you have used an oil-base varnish or paint. Since most decoupage paint is water base—and with this your brush can be cleaned in soap and water—the brush cleaner is used to clean a brush after varnishing. Usually, your brush is just kept in the cleaner the whole time you are doing a decoupage piece. That is, of course, when you are not using it. The cleaner keeps the brush moist, clean, and soft and ready for the next coat of varnish.

Mineral spirits, paint thinner, and turpentine are all referred to as brush cleaners. Pure turpentine is rarely used for decoupage work as it is quite costly and has a very strong odor. Paint thinner or mineral spirits cost about half as much and have only a slight odor. They also don't evaporate as quickly. However, when you leave your brush standing in mineral spirits for any length of time a white gooky substance forms in the solvent. This can easily be cleaned off by running your brush under hot water and wiping it clean.

A soft pastel oriental design was used for this box by Shirley Appy.

Antiquing mix

Brush cleaners have another use. By mixing one third parts of solvent, linseed oil, and an all-purpose or oil-base pigment, you can make your own antiquing mix. The pigment comes in any desirable color in a tube and is purchased in a craft or art supply store. For instance, if you want an earth color antiquing shade, you would buy a burnt sienna or a raw umber.

Boiled linseed oil combined with turpentine and an oil-base pigment in equal parts produces the perfect consistency for the antiquing mix that is applied after your piece has been varnished. If you add a few drops of varnish to this mixture, it will help the antiquing mix to dry more quickly.

Pure linseed oil is generally used in refinishing furniture. When added to pure turpentine it is applied to a wood surface that has been sanded smooth and cleaned. This mixture is then rubbed into the wood and produces a rich color ranging from yellow to reddish brown, depending on the wood.

If you are doing a lot of antiquing, it makes sense to buy your materials and make your own. However, a tiny drop of antiquing goes a long way, so if you only have a small piece to do, it is more economical to buy the antiquing pre-mixed. This is available in small quantities from craft shops and often hardware stores. A quick note: If you decide to buy linseed oil for one reason or another, don't get confused and buy raw linseed oil. This kind takes a lifetime to dry. Some refinishers claim it never does. It is the boiled kind that you want.

Where to find
decoupage prints

It is probably an accurate statement to say that decoupage is a recycling craft. Save, save, save! When you receive a birthday card, take a real good look at it. Maybe you can't use the whole thing for decoupage, but perhaps one leaf from a flower, a border, or some tiny thing is usable. Carefully unwrap your presents. That same paper may be used for a gift that you, in turn, give in the form of decoupage. Posters are inexpensive for large pieces of furniture and there are so many everywhere you go that you really have a terrific selection.

In my last book I had a chapter called "Any Magazine Won't Do." Well, I find that as you grow older and possibly wiser you have the advantage of being able to change your mind. Not completely, but under certain circumstances. However, just to cover my tracks so that you will continue to believe in me, that book was written for beginners primarily, and if you are a beginner I would still say, "Watch out for magazines."

Now that I've confessed my shortcomings (oh, if that were all) I'd like to tell you that while there are some magazines that are usable, it is best to tread cautiously in this area. If there is a lot of print on the back of the design and the paper is thin, the print will often show through when varnished. Sometimes the paper rips when gluing the design in place.

Magazines can be used, but they really aren't good enough. Occasionally I will use a bit of design from a magazine if I run across something that is unusual. However, on a whole the paper is not good enough, the print often smears when varnished, and the material isn't really adaptable in design for decoupage. When you put a lot of time into something it is nicer if it is more original. The magazine designs that I used are applied to inexpensive items for novelty use, such as cans for catchalls.

I've saved my favorite source for last. Books! Do you realize how many books are sitting in cartons in attics all over this country? Well I don't know either, but I can certainly guess that the figure must be in the millions. A great deal more of my time than I'd like to admit has been spent going to tag sales, garage sales, thrift shops, antique shops, dumpyards, auctions, and just plain old poking about. One conclusion I've come to is that people generally collect an awful lot of junk, far more than any junk user can use up in a lifetime. But more importantly, everyone has one thing in common—books. For whatever reason, everywhere you go it is possible to get your hands on books, and if you look through enough of them, you will find the best decoupage material you can get.

Bookstores have sales all the time if you are looking for specific subjects. But if you begin to look for books with good color illustrations, you can start to collect a selection of ideas for later projects. Children's books are often discarded when the kids outgrow them. These often have good color illustrations and even new are inexpensive.

For those of you who have been doing decoupage for some time and are looking for more elegant designing material, fine prints are exciting to work with. These are expensive—usually $10 or more—and often difficult to find. I usually go to galleries or fine bookstores. There you will find hand-colored engravings, lithographs, and often lovely black-and-white prints. These should be used for something special and only on a well-made box or similar object, such as a fine piece of furniture.

When I was working on my design book, *Decoupage Designs,* Jon and I decided to add some very special prints. Since most of the prints we were using were flowers and mushrooms and whimsical characters, our only predetermined idea was to try to find subjects that were different, yet still traditional in feeling. We visited many art galleries and print shops most of which are found only in fairly good-

Lap desk made by Gramp, decoupaged by Ruth Linsley.

sized cities. Those in small towns usually don't carry a large enough variety of hand-colored prints. Surprisingly, we found few that we felt were nice enough to use. However, the few that we did find we felt were exceptional. Some are of birds, a couple of flower prints (it is hard to keep me away from the flower subjects), and one that I really loved of an old-world sphere on a stand in the most exquisite brown colors.

One of the prints we found was a bouquet of flowers in blues with touches of pink. It was really quite elegant. Another was of a bunch of cherries. This print was quite large and so beautiful that I couldn't bear to cut it apart. Instead I had it framed and gave it to Jon for Christmas. Often the trouble with finding really beautiful prints is that they are too lovely to cut into. It is nice to know, however, that they do exist.

Craft shops are becoming better equipped, and these are good places to find a range of subjects all packaged so that you can buy one of a certain subject. This eliminates the need for buying a complete book of birds if you only need one bird.

Wallpaper is usually not used for decoupage, although I did use it for one project that is described later on. The reason for not using wallpaper is that the paper is so absorbent it takes too many coats of varnish to cover it. Also, since it is generally thick, it is difficult to cut out designs so that they are neat and sharp. But because of its thickness wallpaper is excellent for lining boxes.

Fabric is also not for decoupage. It is difficult to cut the designs, the fabric ravels, and the varnish discolors the material. This is not decoupage anyway, since the decoupage process is creating a design from cutout paper.

Photographs can be used for decoupage. Both black-and-white and color have been used successfully. Use them as is or cut up in a collage as I did with mine.

Embossed or raised paper is not especially good for decoupage because it cannot be glued down flat and when covered with varnish does not become submerged as the rest of the design does.

Keep in mind that there is much more that can be used than can't for decoupage; save things and keep your eyes open for new and interesting designs.

I do not recommend coloring your own prints as there is such a variety of already printed sources for you to select from that I don't feel this is necessary. I recognize that the art of coloring prints is indeed an art still practiced by many, but I can't see its importance. Years and years ago, before modern printing techniques were perfected there was a reason to hand color prints, but now color printing has been perfected to such a degree that to me it seems silly to bother. (Oh, I can see the letters of disgust pouring in now.) However, I stand firm. If you enjoy hand coloring and would like to do it for fun, why not? But with so much available to the decoupage craftsperson I think it is more fun to design with the other materials I've mentioned. There is just so much variety.

There is no substitute for cuticle scissors

I hate to be so dogmatic, but that's the way it is. Call them what you will (some refer to them as decoupage scissors), but the very best type of scissors to use is the regular cuticle scissors that can be purchased in a drugstore. This curved scissors can't be beaten for cutting in and out of all the tiny curves you're bound to run into sooner or later. If you buy Revlon scissors, which cost about $4.00, and they break or wear out, Revlon will replace or repair them for $1.00, so in a sense these scissors are guaranteed for life. There is also a better grade of cuticle scissors made of stainless steel. They are found in craft or notion shops and cost approximately $10.

When cutting something large, like a poster or anything that requires straight cutting, I use a regular sewing scissors, but this is the only time. I find that embroidery scissors, although small, do not work as well and give you choppy cuts rather than nice smooth rounded cuts. This is particularly important when cutting around petals and leaves. Once you have your scissors, take good care of them and only use them for cutting paper, not cuticles or nails. And no, you can't do even one decoupage project with a razor blade, or worse yet kitchen scissors. If you want to do a great job, this is not the way. You can use the leftover living room paint, but please not old scissors.

Using a tack cloth

A tack cloth is generally used for wiping off the dust from sanding before continuing to paint or varnish. These cloths can be purchased in paint and hardware stores as well as most automotive parts stores. If you want to make one yourself, soak a piece of cheesecloth with varnish, ring it out, and then keep it in a tightly closed jar so that it remains sticky. When used, this picks up all the dust on your piece. To tell the truth, I never use one simply because I don't like the whole idea. The feel of the sticky cloth is unappealing to me. A nice soft diaper or undershirt is my favorite for dusting a piece, but I thought you might like to know what a tack cloth is just in case someone brings it up at a party or somewhere. And it has a nice ring to it, and when you mention it you have to admit it does sound as though you are not one to argue with about the ins and outs of refinishing or decoupage. A paper towel is too full of lint to use effectively, but in emergencies and for lack of something better I have been known to use one. However, I'm sure you will

Tiny designs are used on this dollhouse dresser.

be more organized than I am and will have all the necessary materials before starting. Too often I find myself up to my elbows in antiquing before yelling, "Quick, someone hand me a towel." That's how I end up using paper towels.

Wax

I tried very hard to think of a catchy title for this section. Wax is so plain, but then again it is direct. When your piece is finished a coat of wax is applied to give it a warm

Each section of this display unit was lined with different wallpaper samples. Displayed are decoupaged crayon cups, stamp dispenser, and napkin rings.

glow and to protect it. I use a furniture paste wax such as Johnson's or Butcher's Bowling Alley Wax, both of which can be found in hardware and automotive parts stores or supermarkets. The can gives you directions on how to use, although I'm sure every man, woman, or child reading this knows the procedure for applying wax and then rubbing it off. I'm told nobody polishes furniture anymore, but even if you don't polish furniture, you will find this an easy procedure.

So there you are. That's your list of supplies and where to find everything. Many of the items you may already own, but even so, if there is a craft shop near you, it will be fun to look through what they offer. As you proceed with decoupage and increase your knowledge about the craft you will be able to judge for yourself which of these supplies you want, so you should know what is available.

I'll be discussing all these materials further as we get into the projects. This is simply a buying guide, but now that you've invested the money you will have to stick with me to find out what to do with all those materials.

Decoupage processes: learning by doing

If you don't like radishes

Some people don't like radishes. As a matter of fact, they find them downright ugly, to say nothing of their taste. So maybe you didn't like the radish plaque I did. That's O.K. You'll be motivated to come up with a better idea.

But isn't it about time we got started with something meaningful? Rather than start with an easy project and work gradually up to something super terrific that takes months, I thought I'd show you projects that are fun to do, yet include all the techniques you need to know. Some are small and can be squeezed in between larger projects; some won't appeal to you at all, and some will seem altogether silly (a decoupaged boat?). But the projects I'm going to show you will teach you some new aspect of decoupage. For instance, if you want to learn about varnishing for outdoors so that you can do your mailbox, then you can find the information under the sailboat project. If you want to stain rather than paint, you'll find it under "an undressed dresser." My intention is not to bore you with long paragraphs on how to hold the sandpaper correctly. As a trial-and-error craftsperson in training you'll learn it all as we go along from one project to the next. Doing is learning.

One summer
in Nantucket

There is a children's book that I have always loved. It is called *One Summer in Maine* by Robert McCloskey. When I read it, it gave me a good feeling, and I could imagine exactly what it would be like to live there. I guess I've come close to knowing that experience by spending my summers on Nantucket, except that Nantucket is more populated than Robert McCloskey's corner of Maine seemed to be. Because I've always liked the book, and since the next project was done during one summer in Nantucket, I hope Mr. McCloskey will forgive me for using his title with a slight change to the ending.

Let's start from the beginning with how a project "happens." Some tag sales are really awful. There is usually lots of junk that is overpriced and should have been carted away with the trash. Others have just the thing you were looking for—last year. But once in a great while you discover just the thing you didn't know you had to have.

Jon and I are avid tag or garage sale followers and run to every sale and auction around. We call them tag sales in New England. Perhaps they are called by different names in other sections of the country. This is a sale of "stuff" that someone wants to get rid of after doing a major house cleaning. The person puts everything out on the lawn or tags it all in the garage. The items typically range from old cribs to furniture, glassware, etc. Things that are no longer of value to the owner, but may be what a neighbor will buy for a small cost. One person's throw-away is another's treasure.

At any rate, since Jon and I are downright afraid that if we miss one, it will be the very one that has all the treasures, we usually hit ten dreadful sales for every good one. Maybe we waste a lot of Saturday and Sunday afternoons, but how can you know beforehand? We are fortunate to live in New England where acquiring and getting rid of "junk/antiques" is the local pastime. We usually don't have any predetermined idea of what we're after, and are guided only by our native Yankee ingenuity that tells us, "Get it as cheaply as possible or don't get it at all." When it comes to prints, I often pay dearly for them, but having been spoiled by my grandfather who has made my boxes for years, I find it hard to pay a lot for something that is made poorly. There are still some great buys around, and if you are fairly flexible and keep in mind that decoupage can make some rather ugly things beautiful, you can actually find a bargain or two.

One Saturday morning we read in the paper about a tag sale that a local sign company was having. We couldn't imagine what they could have that we might want. (Probably a bunch of neon signs), but we went anyway. It turned out to be one of the best sales we've ever found. As a matter of fact, we were so carried away that we almost forgot that old Yankee rule. There was everything from old stained glass church windows to neon signs of long ago. Losing your head is easy in such situations, and unfortunately neither of us is the sensible one who keeps pulling the other away. Together we almost walked out of there with a $35 neon sign that flashed "Coca-Cola" in shocking pink. Fortunately, we didn't have thirty-five dollars between us or we wouldn't have eaten that week.

But we did find in the yard outside of the store a small child's desk and chair. These were not attached, but were the kind that screwed to the floor of the classroom. The size was good—not too large—and I thought they were worth every bit of the ten dollars I paid. I have since learned that many people own desks like this one. If you have something similar, you might think of decoupaging it. Now's the time to bring it out of the basement and back into use. Perhaps it can become a gift or a piece to set the phone on in the hallway. Mine ended up in a gallery. If you don't have a similar piece of furniture, the process and designing techniques I used can be applied to another piece that you might have. If you find something that has interesting lines, but is quite beaten up, examine it carefully. Often things look worse than they actually are. Wood putty can be used to fill in holes and gouges, and some distress marks are interesting when accented by antiquing.

A child's desk and chair are great pieces of furniture to decoupage, mostly because they are small in scale and present a variety of challenges. The flat surface of the desk is easy enough to design and yet it does have areas—around the inkwell, along the top ridge, and even in the pencil holder groove—that can be treated in interesting ways.

The chair, like the desk surface, is functional, and the design really shouldn't cover the seat. The rungs are another area of concern, not only in the painting and refinishing, but in the area of design. My immediate thought when I see chair rungs is toward vines or ivy or delicate flowers winding their way around them.

An old school desk and chair make an interesting project.

When I first spot a piece that I want to work on, I begin to visualize the design. However, it isn't until I have really gotten the feel of the piece that I start to experiment, and usually the final look is entirely different from what I first visualized. It is a whole process that happens when you begin to create something with your own hands and body and mind. It is this process which repeats itself over and over that keeps the creativity flowing. Many times I am asked, "Don't you get tired of decoupage? Of doing the same thing over and over again?" Well, I never really do. Each time I start a new project the same feeling of excitement comes over me and I can't wait to see the finished project emerge. It is with this renewed feeling of excitement that I discovered the little old desk and chair shoved aside among many pieces of junk at the tag sale. I can't explain what makes that one object jump out and make you say, "This is exactly what I want," but it really does happen and you'll know when it does.

The desk and chair sat in my barn in Westport for over a month before we dusted it off and got ready to take it with us for the summer.

Along with the dog, kids, and lots and lots of art supplies, Jon and I loaded the desk and chair into the car for the trip to Nantucket. (And it isn't a station wagon either.) A week after we arrived and everyone settled down to a lazy summer routine, I began to strip the desk and chair. The pieces were badly marked and scratched and the metal bases were very rusty. The first thing that should be done when you are going to refinish a piece of furniture is to clean it completely so that you can see what you've got to work with. This can be done with turpentine and a clean rag. Sometimes on small things like boxes I don't bother to strip the finish, although on a piece of furniture it will hold up better if you do. Now, if you don't want to bother stripping, the first thing to do after it has been cleaned is to sand the piece with a heavy sandpaper. You can paint right over everything once it is sanded smooth.

An electric sander can be used to remove rust or paint.

There is a quick test you can make to find out what kind of finish a piece of furniture has so you will know how to remove it. If you are planning to do it from scratch, the way I have, it can be fun, and you will learn a lot as well as gain a feeling of satisfaction from doing such a project. Since this was a school desk from many years ago, chances are the finish would not be varnish, but shellac. To test whether or not your piece has a shellac finish, pour a little denatured alcohol on the top as I did with the desk. If

*Sanding block makes
holding sandpaper easier.*

*Alcohol will remove a
shellac finish.*

*Use a scraper to remove
the finish after applying
the alcohol.*

within seconds the finish begins to dissolve, it is shellac. As I thought, the desk had a shellac finish. Since the finish had been there for a long time it took much alcohol and time to remove the shellac. But there is nothing particularly difficult about this procedure. First of all, let me warn you that the alcohol you use is definitely *not* the kind you drink. I thought I should clarify that. It is important to buy "Denatured Alcohol" since it is the only thing that will dissolve shellac. Paint remover can be used as a substitute for the alcohol, but I find it is much harder to work with, and it does not dissolve the finish so easily. So don't let them fool you at the hardware or paint store. Buy the alcohol no matter what the salesman tells you. Another important note, never use alcohol in a closed room. It absorbs moisture in the room and will make you feel dizzy. If it's nice weather, do this outside or open all windows and doors when using it inside. Now you know why I work in Nantucket. Besides, I'm very messy.

Simply pour the alcohol right on the piece of furniture and spread it around either with a brush or a clean rag. A brush is better because the rag absorbs a lot of the liquid that you want to seep into the shellac. The shellac finish should start to dissolve right away. Obviously, this is one messy job, and I did all the work in the back yard. If it's winter or you live in an apartment, cover the floor with lots of newspaper before you begin.

Using a paint scraper (available in a hardware or paint store), scrape off the finish as it begins to dissolve. It comes off in big glops. Remove as much of the finish as possible so that there is little left to sand off. Alcohol evaporates quickly so it is best to work on a small section at a time. If the alcohol is left on for too long the shellac becomes gummy and hard to remove. Another method is to pour the alcohol on and then scrub it with a piece of steel wool. The steel wool replaces the scraper. I suggest you wear rubber gloves, although I imagine you gave up long ago on having nicely manicured nails. It is impossible in this decoupage business.

I had decided to go right down to the original bare wood but hand sanding can be time-consuming and would have taken much time away from the sun and beach. What I'm going to confess to next will probably shock many purists of the art of refinishing and decoupage. So if you shock easily, read no further.

I used an electric sander. Not the super-powerful kind that is strictly for flat sanding—that would have been too difficult for getting around the rungs of the chair and into crevices. I bought sanding discs and attached a circular sanding piece to the electric hand drill that we just happened to have brought with us along with everything else. (I am told it's no fun traveling in a car for four hours with an electric sander straddled between your legs, but I feel everyone can sacrifice a little.)

An alcohol-soaked rag can be used for the rungs.

The sanding attachment is available in any hardware store and is a very convenient tool to own. It is truly an exciting feeling when using a sander to watch the beautiful clean wood emerge as the old finish is magically whirred away. I happen to love using an electric sander because the combination of the smell of the sanded wood and the sight of the transformation really thrills me. Even so, there is still a lot of hand sanding required for a project like the desk and chair. All the rungs have to be finished by hand and inside the inkwell and the pencil ridge. As you work on an old piece like this you can imagine a little girl sitting at the desk dipping her pen into the inkwell.

If you don't have an electric sander, all sanding must be done by hand. The 3M Company recently came out with a lightweight plastic sanding block that you might look for. Confidentially, I think that I rushed the job of applying alcohol because I love using the electric sander so much. If you really stick with the alcohol bath and the steel wool, there should be no need to sand your piece at all, except to smooth things out at the end.

Hand sand the chair rungs to remove the finish.

If you find that you have a lot of rust on your object, as I did with the base of this desk and chair, there are commercial rust removers on the market. I didn't find one that was really satisfactory and ended up removing as much as I could off the base of the chair with the sander. After sanding the desk and chair a little bit each day (between bike trips to the beach) I let Jon add a little of his labor. Naturally, after a couple of minutes of sanding a neighbor came by and commented, "Nice job you've done there, Jon." Oh well, a gold star wasn't what I was after anyway. Once all the electric sanding was completed, I went over the whole thing by hand with a fine sandpaper such as 3M "Wetordry" super-fine #400. When there was no shellac left on the pieces anywhere, they were ready to be painted.

For all small decoupage projects, like boxes and plaques, I recommend water-base paints. These might be the latex or acrylic paints found in your local craft shops as I described earlier. However, when doing a piece of furniture I have found that it is best to use an oil enamel paint, which produces a harder, longer-lasting finish.

After you have stripped your furniture to the bare wood, you must apply a paint sealer. This should also be applied to unfinished furniture that you buy commercially. The sealer is used so that your paint won't be absorbed into the wood. Instead, the sealer penetrates into the wood fibers and dries to a hard tough finish on which to work. After the sealer has dried it should be rubbed down with a fine steel wool or sandpaper. When applying the sealer and the paint do not do anything with the metal base if there is one. Leave this part until last.

Once the sealer dries (twenty-four hours) and is sanded you are ready to paint. Select a flat enamel in the color of your choice. The sealer is usually white, but any color paint can be applied over it. I used a white enamel for my finish because I wanted it to look like ivory. The coats of varnish that are applied change the flat white to a soft ivory finish that is quite elegant.

Applying paint

You must be careful in selecting the color paint you will use. As I said, flat white turns ivory under varnish. Pink is a terrible color for decoupage, because it usually turns orange under the varnish. It is true that you use a clear varnish, but I have never used an oil-base varnish that does not have a touch of orange in it. The water-base varnishes, which are polymer medium, are clear, but for furniture you need an oil-base varnish, so you might as well know the facts. Pale blue will usually turn slightly green. Yellow is an excellent color, as is mustard, green—if it is not too dark—and burnt orange. Actually, I prefer the pastel colors because the designs stand out better than on a dark background. However, I once used a deep red for an oriental design and I liked the result. But my mother once used black for a background color, and I must say I thought it was awful.

I use a polyfoam brush to paint furniture because I want to avoid brush strokes as much as possible. When working with a large surface and with enamel it is hard to avoid brush strokes that dry in ridges. The surface is so hard when dry that it is very difficult to sand them flat once you've got them. Your brush should be cleaned in mineral spirits or turpentine. This kind of brush can only be used with paint or varnish, not shellac or lacquer as these chemicals will dissolve the foam rubber.

When painting be sure that your paint is mixed well. Shake it well before using. Two coats of paint should cover nicely. The procedure is really quite simple. Dip your brush into the paint and wipe off the excess on the inside of the can. Starting in the middle of your flat surface, draw your brush toward the outer edges. The reason for starting in the middle is to eliminate what is known as "roll over." It's not a contagious disease, but is the build-up of excess paint around the edge of your piece where too much has accumulated. The paint should be evenly spread over the surface. All painting should be done in one direction, with the grain of the wood. After you have applied the paint to the entire surface go back over the area in the opposite direction without adding more paint to your brush. This time, how-

A flat enamel paint is used for this project.

ever, the brush should only touch very lightly on the painted surface. This will help smooth your paint job. Now, using the tip of your brush and with an even lighter touch go back the other way again. The hardest thing for me to teach in decoupage is to use a delicate hand. I find most people sand harder or glop on paint more freely than necessary. Lightly, please. Tread lightly.

Another thing to watch for in painting is dripping. If you overload your brush you will have drip marks that, once dry, are impossible to sand off. You will end up scraping them off with a razor blade which is a messy job, so try to be careful. It is important to have an even paint job, especially when you are working on such a large surface. It is far less critical when working on a plaque or box that will have most of the surface covered. However, in any project the better the painting, the better your finish will be.

One thing I should remind you of is that when painting or sanding the rungs of a chair you have to take a bit more care than with a flat surface. It is easiest to sand turned or curved areas, such as the rungs, by cutting the sandpaper in strips. Hold each end and work the paper back and forth in the grooves or over the curved out areas. When painting these parts do it carefully without loading your brush with paint. This will avoid drips drying hard on the rungs.

When using enamel paint each coat must dry overnight at room temperature. Our house in Nantucket is very tiny, and the only possible place for the desk and chair was in the living room. Easier said than done. With two full days just for the paint to dry, a previous day of sealer drying and still many days of varnish drying to go, I was rapidly becoming very unpopular in our house. Friends must have wondered about my sanity when they saw a chair piled onto the only table in the room surrounded by a barricade of chairs. Or the kids getting their meals shoved to them through the open door.

When the pieces are finally dry they must be sanded between coats so that the surfaces will be as smooth as possible. I rarely use a heavy sandpaper. The fine black sandpaper mentioned previously can be used and if wet slightly will produce a lovely smooth base for your work. By the way, I did not paint the inside of the desk because I planned to line it with wallpaper when I finished.

Decoupage
designs

We've finally come to the part of decoupage that is my favorite, so I will try not to get carried away, but I warn you it is a challenge. I've already given you some ideas for where to find subjects to cut up for your own decoupage designs. But what you want to know is how *do* you design. That's something that you really do learn from looking and doing. Obviously, some people are more creative than others, but all people have a feeling for what they like. And that's all there is to it. What makes a good design is when you look at your piece and like it. But how do you get started? Start by thumbing through some books, magazines, and cards. Think of a favorite subject, hobby, place, or person. If you just take a little time to clear your head, you'll start to come up with ideas.

Here are a few simple ones: Take the month you were born and use your flower for a central theme. Do you like to go fishing? Use different fish on a box. If you go boating, perhaps signal flags could be used. I've seen books on everything from old cars to wild flowers to almost anything that anyone collects. They aren't big expensive art books either, but inexpensive full-color paperbacks. Start with an idea that is quite simple and before you know it you will have added little animals under a tree with the flower of the month at the base, and started to create a scene. Some might design a fantasy story and others something quite sophisticated.

Whatever you design, you should take your time because this is the most important part of your work. When your box is ultimately sitting on a coffee table to be admired, the first thing that people will notice is your design, not how many coats of varnish you've applied. Of course, we all should strive for the perfect finish, much as the surfer strives for the perfect wave, but that's secondary. First, let's look good. As we go along from project to project you will get more of a feeling for designing different sized and shaped items and using different kinds of materials. I'm sure you'll come up with all sorts of additional ideas.

A woman in one of my classes once told me that she felt that decoupage had opened up a whole new way of viewing things. She said that going places and doing ordinary things were more enjoyable because she always had an eye out for decoupage ideas. What a wonderful thing to have happen to you. I feel this way about my craft, and I think once you get into it you will too.

In another of my classes in Nantucket I met a girl who was about thirteen. She was designing a box with one of my prints that had a Dutch boy in wooden shoes dancing opposite a squirrel dressed in a little red suit. At least when I used the print I saw them dancing. This young person looked at it, cut out the boy only, turned him slightly so that his feet were out in front of him and said she saw him in the midst of falling. For the first time I saw how cute this would be, but it was her idea and this design became her original creation. She made it the way she saw it, and this wasn't something I could have given her. I wish we had photographed it, but she left the island before we had a chance.

Everyone looks at designs differently. I usually like to make fantasy scenes with large flowers and tiny creatures here and there. Sometimes you have to look carefully at one of my boxes to find them. For instance, it is fun to camouflage bugs. Whenever I have long grass stems or branches I will try to find a caterpiller that I can place crawling up the stem. If it is the same color, it will be subtle enough that one will have to look twice to see it. It is nice to discover something new in a piece when you look at it a second time. On the other hand, if you make a box that is subtle in design and color—say white flowers on a white box with only green stems for color—it is often interesting to add a butterfly with just a drop of color in its wings. Perhaps you can pick up this touch of color, say orange, in the lining. It is a grand surprise to open a delicately designed box only to find a brilliant color on the inside.

When choosing a design you should be thinking about the color of the background first. The paint and the choosing of the cutouts usually go hand and hand because they are, of course, related to one another. You wouldn't paint the box or plaque, etc., and then go out to look for your print; these decisions should be made together. Shape also affects your decision about cutouts. If you're working on a very flat square surface, you must first decide if, for instance, you want to use a symmetrical design or something that is free-flowing, such as viney flowers. I particularly love daisies because they are informal, grow wild, and are so young and uninhibited in feeling. Usually I use a curved top box for these beauties because the shape is not stiff. Later on when I show you how to make an address oval or use my pumpkins

Now that you know generally what to look for in design let's more specifically relate design to the project at hand, in this case the desk and chair. I wanted to have a design that was young and airy in feeling, but not childish, so I didn't want to use children's pictures. I saw it as a piece not necessarily for a child, but rather as an object by itself and wanted it to have a more sophisticated look. I usually don't do that because I like art that is functional, but I don't always like to use things for what they are obviously intended either.

Earlier in June of that year, when we had gone up to Nantucket for a weekend, I had purchased a beautiful book on birds—an oversized art book done by an artist in Canada. He had taken real stuffed birds, placed them on branches from their natural habitat and painted them in this "native" setting. They are exquisite and became my source for the desk and chair. I felt the brilliant red and orange colors against the ivory background would look striking with the soft green leaves.

Whenever possible the designs for one piece should all come from the same source, so that they will be of the same value in color, printing, and weight. If the paper is of different weights, you will need more varnish on the thicker paper, and when you feel the finish it will not be even. Also, if the colors are not exactly compatible, they won't complement each other. These may seem like small points, but they are important if the piece is to look professional.

Cutting

Often I will cut out prints that I think will go well together on a particular piece only to find that once cut out and laid in place, they don't work at all. Sometimes you just have to cut them out to tell. Don't consider this wasted time since you can always use the cutouts on something else. You will achieve better results if you don't use everything just because you have already cut them out.

When you cut, have the point of your cuticle scissors curved away rather than toward the cutout. This will give you more control over your cutting. If you have the curve turned inward, you are more apt to lop off a leaf or bud as you cut.

Cut as close to the design as possible. Try not to leave a white edge around your piece. Particularly if you are to place the pieces on a background other than white, you will not want the white edges showing off a bad cutting job. Yes, you must get the little places in between stems and so forth. I wish I had a penny for all the times I've been asked, "Do I have to cut out all the tiny places?" This is decoupage, remember? The art of designing with paper CUTOUTS! And you'll be so glad you took the extra time.

Apart from the above caution, there is no special way to cut except to do it the way it feels right to you. A few hints might be helpful, however. If you're cutting a very lacy print, one with lots of stems and leaves and buds, it is easiest if you cut from the inside toward the outer edges rather than

Assemble cutouts before planning final design.

Use the sharp point of your cuticle scissors to refine the cutting of detailed areas.

Hold scissors curved away from design for a professional cutting job.

the reverse. This way while you are cutting out all the little hard-to-get-at places you will have the outer edge of the print to hold on to. Also, when cutting very skinny stems with flowers on the end, you should cut the flowering part first. This way you don't have a lacy, delicate stem holding a top-heavy weight of excess paper. Between cutting sessions keep the cut pieces safely between the pages of a book. A book will hold them in place ready to use without danger of tearing or spoiling.

If you keep your prints and scissors handy, you can cut during otherwise "wasted" time. I keep mine by the telephone so that I can cut while talking. You can also do your cutting while stuck in traffic. It is a great way to take wasted time and make it work for you. Waiting for baseball practice to let out, cut. If you're a commuter, after a bit of practice you can even learn to cut on the train.

Arranging prints

This is the part that is really designing. In a sense it's much like arranging a bouquet of flowers—something I'm not too good at so I suppose it is a bad comparison. But for lack of a better one, I'll use it. Lay all the pieces that you've cut out on your piece and push them around a bit. Try them in different ways. Eliminate some. Try to decide if you need more. Never just start with one, glue it on, add another, and so on. That's like painting yourself into a corner. You get all done only to find that you are left with a gaping space and nothing that will fit. Oh, you've already done that? Well, let's try again.

First put all the cutout pieces in position the way you think they look best. This is the only way you will be able to tell if you need a bit more here and there. Take the time to find exactly what you think is needed. If it's a leaf to fill in space or to add to another branch, don't settle for any leaf. Be sure it is the exact size and shape that you want. After all there are plenty of leaves in the pond. Be selective. If you merely settle for a mediocre design, you won't feel the same kind of excitement as the piece develops.

Once you are satisfied with the design you are ready to glue the pieces in place. Take each cutout off one at a time, glue it, and place it back in position before picking up another piece. This is easy with a flat surface, but what about those rungs on the chair? What if you want trailing ivy wrapped around each one? If the surface isn't flat, you have to improvise. I usually just hold it up to see if it's "right," stamp it in my memory, and plunge forth. If you don't feel this confident or foolish, you can put a drop of rubber cement on the back of the design and then place it where you want to look at it. A cheaper solution is a kneaded eraser

Plan your design carefully before gluing.

which you can buy in an art supply or stationery store. Just put a teeny spot of the eraser on the object and press the design to it. As I write this those procedures sound like more trouble than they are worth, so unless you're super insecure why don't you just try it my way.

Gluing: after this
there's no undoing

That's right! Once it's in place you can kiss that cutout good-bye. There is no way to correct mistakes here, so you've got to be pretty darn sure before putting glue to paper. At least with my method there's no undoing. If you've come across a way, I'd like to hear from you, but don't write and tell me about rubber cement—that's not decoupage gluing. What we are dealing with here is a permanent bond. You can make many mistakes in your life and undo them. You can form a permanent bond in marriage that might turn out not to be so permanent, and you can undo it. But a decoupage bond is for life!

A white paper glue is best for decoupage, such as Elmer's Glue-All, Sobo, or a glue that is similar. Recently the Borden company came out with Arts and Crafts glue that I have

A delicate piece can be cut apart and then glued to the object one piece at a time. This will keep it from ripping.

The heavy leaf and berry are attached by a delicate stem. This can be cut away and glued back in place separately so that it will look perfectly natural.

been testing. It is stickier than the Glue-All and dries clear and fast. What its long-range effect will be I can't say, but for the moment at least I still like old-fashioned Elmer's. When decoupaging on metal the white glue is impossible because you are working with a nonporous material. For these projects I use 3M Super Strength glue.

Have a clean sponge ready beside you when gluing. It should be slightly damp, but not wet. Before beginning you might want to check over your designs once again. If any of the cutouts are lacy and delicate, the glue could rip them apart. To prevent this, I sometimes cut the print apart in spots where, when glued in place on the object, you cannot tell that it was ever in two pieces. Also, be sure your hands are clean so that the cutout won't get stuck to your fingers instead of the object.

Take one cutout off the desk—or whatever you are working on—and turn it over on a gluing board. This surface could be anything—a piece of window pane glass is perfect, the top of a formica counter top, or a piece of lucite or ceramic. But don't do your gluing on a piece of paper, for the glue makes the cutout stick to the paper and you can lose part of it when lifting it off. Since the white glue is easily cleaned off with water, you can do your gluing right on the kitchen counter if you like. However, the Super Strength glue must be cleaned with nail polish remover, so is best used with a special board.

Squirt a drop of glue in the center of the cutout and use your finger to spread it to all outer edges. It should be spread evenly.

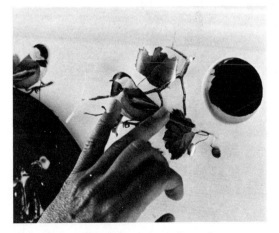

Your fingers should not be full of glue when placing the design on your object. Press down firmly on your design.

Squirt a drop of glue in the center of the cutout and using your fingertip spread it around to the outer edges. It should be evenly spread and not overloaded. Clean your fingers quickly and then carefully pick up the design. Lay it in place on the project, and with the palm of your hand press it down firmly. Using the sponge, dab at the entire thing to remove any excess glue. Then with a clean pencil or brush handle roll over the freshly glued design to force any extra

Using the brush handle, roll over the design to ooze excess glue out of the edges.

You may want to lengthen a branch. Cut the new piece so that it will look natural when added.

Glue the new piece in place so that the design is extended the way it looks best.

Using a damp sponge, pat over entire design to remove any excess glue that may be on the surface.

When half of your planned
design is glued in place
stand back and take a look
at the whole thing.

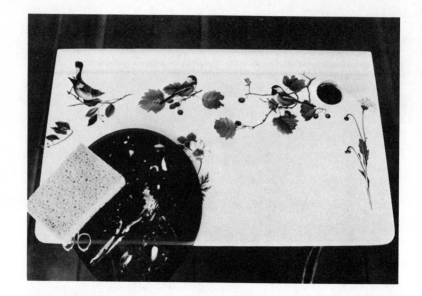

The dandelion stem at the
far right was extended by
adding a piece with a leaf
from something else. In
this way the flower starts
at the bottom of the desk,
and the bud remains up
near the inkwell.

The long dandelion on the
left balances the design on
the right. The center is
left free of design so that
the desk can be used.

glue to ooze out of the edges. This step will also insure that all edges are glued down firmly which is important because the varnish will cause the design to lift if it gets underneath it. Most people find this hard to believe since the varnish is so sticky. However, if it seeps under the design it will dry in a lump, thus raising the design at that point. Ultimately, you will be able to peel it off.

Repeat this process of gluing and pressing down the cut-outs until most of the plan for the overall design is completed. Then stand back and take a look at the whole thing. Does it need a piece added here or there where it wasn't apparent before?

With the desk I tried to make the design go up the sides and across the top and avoided the center surface. This way the desk can be used. If the design covered the desk top, it would have been impossible to write on it. If you are doing a similar piece of furniture, you might want to add even more designs that would flow onto the sides and front. I held back with this design, and only used one bird on a branch, picking up the orange color, on the front of the desk. I had even more trouble with the chair and suspect that chairs are a difficult design problem. I have since done two more chairs (different shapes), and they also have presented me with design difficulties. As with the desk, the design didn't cover the main area of the chair which would, of course, be covered when sitting.

When designing the chair I picked up the theme from the desk but added a few touches of whimsy here and there with just a small design on the back. There are a million ways that this project could have been done, and though I'm not sure that mine was the best, I like it.

I did have a horrid experience with this desk project, however. I was rushing to get enough pieces finished for a show that I was to have in a local gallery. Now, if you are a painter and are faced with filling a gallery with paintings it is one thing, but to fill an entire gallery with decoupage boxes is something else again. Yes, an entire room! I really wanted to have a couple of larger pieces so that my tiny boxes wouldn't look so puny. The desk and chair were to be my centerpiece. I had my varnishing schedule all planned out, including, of course, compensation for typically wet Nantucket days. During the week before the show I had to fly to New York and my parents were coming to Nantucket for the two days. My mother was going to add coats of varnish to the desk while I was gone. Just before leaving I

When you have a very fragile cutout you can apply the glue right to the surface of the desk to avoid tearing the design when applying the glue.

As you lay the design onto the glue spread the glue out with your brush as you hold the design away.

Dab the excess glue away with a damp sponge. Be sure all glue is wiped away before applying varnish.

applied a coat of varnish over the surface of the desk and placed it by the window to dry. It was a warm, dry day when we flew out of Nantucket airport about fifteen minutes before my mother's plane was due to arrive.

That night I called home from our motel, and after talking awhile about mundane things, I asked my mother the most important question, "How's the desk?" Silence. I persisted and finally she told me that the slight breeze from the window had caused dirt particles to blow through the screen ruining the surface completely. "I can't believe that," I shrieked. Of course, I could believe it, I just refused to. Much more of a perfectionist about varnish jobs than I am, she refused to give me any solace. Not even a shred of hope. "Well, wait until tomorrow and see if you can sand it a bit, then put another coat on," I suggested. "I'll try," was about the only hope I could illicit. The next night I called her again. What was I to do? This was my important piece for the show. "It's not good," she offered.

When we finally got back to Nantucket two days later than expected, I checked the desk knowing that if it was a failure there was nothing I could do but raffle it off amongst the dog and kids as a boobie prize or punishment for some hideous crime like dropping gum wrappers on the front

A little sprig was added to the left top and a bit of design around the inkwell for interest.

lawn. Well, I must admit it wasn't a Leslie Linsley special; on the other hand, it certainly couldn't be compared to the San Francisco earthquake. Some wet sanding and a few more coats of varnish had it looking respectable enough to antique. That is the magic word, antique. Because antiquing, when done well, can hide most mistakes and you come out with mishaps hardly noticeable. More on how to do this later.

What makes a superb finish

Since I've now told you about this great finish we are striving for, how do you achieve it? With a clean brush and new varnish mostly. It is not difficult to varnish a decoupaged piece. You simply dip your brush into the can, wiping the excess off on the inside rim as you draw the brush out. Starting in the middle of the item, you brush from one side to the other so that the varnish becomes thinner as you get to the edges. Then lightly draw your brush back the other way across the surface. And that's it. However, it does take twenty-four hours for a coating to completely dry. Usually the varnish will be set dry in four hours, but you will ruin your project if you varnish on top of a coat that is not absolutely dry. During this drying time the biggest hazard is dust that settles on your piece, especially if it is a large object.

Whether you are after a glossy finish or a satin matte finish, the technique of applying varnish is the same. After the painting is completed, sand the entire piece so that it is smooth and dust free. Be sure to clean off the sand grit with a clean cloth. Apply your cutout design as described previously making sure to remove all excess glue. (I know I went through all this, but my Nantucket story seems to have gotten in the way.)

Dip your brush into the varnish and begin as before. If there is too much varnish applied to the edges of your piece, it will drip down the sides. Also, the varnish can collect at the edges forming a thick yellow ridge, which once dry is impossible to sand smooth and even with the rest of your surface. Be sure that any excess varnish is spread thin. Edges should be varnished with a light hand. A thin coat of varnish is better than a thick one.

Air bubbles often cause bumps in your finish. This can be corrected when you sand after the varnish is dry. Thinning the varnish slightly with a thinner also cuts down on air bubbles. After applying the varnish to a box, I usually hold it up to the light so I can see where I missed. Since varnish is clear it is difficult to see whether you have covered the entire surface unless you varnish against the light. Then with the very tip of your brush pop any air bubbles that you can see. What are left can be sanded smooth after the box is completely dry.

If you can't decide whether to have a glossy or matte finish, don't fret over it. You can try both very simply. When your varnish is dry and it has a very shiny finish you can turn it into a satin finish by rubbing it all over with fine steel wool. On the other hand, if you have applied a satin finish and would like to try the glossy, simply apply a coat of glossy finish right over the matte. Each coat should of course first be dry. One coat completely cancels out the other in terms of dullness or shininess. After the first two coats of varnish, each coat should be sanded lightly before the next coat is applied, so even your glossy finish will not remain quite as glossy as it first appears.

There is nothing like a new can of varnish, but I always try to use everything on hand before succumbing to buying anything new. Even when the varnish gets old and gummy I spend hours straining it through a stocking and adding mineral spirits so I can use the last of it. But I don't recommend this until you have had considerable experience with varnish.

Also, keep in mind that it is best to varnish at room temperature and that it will probably take two days for the varnish to dry if you apply it on a rainy day. Best to wait until the skies are clear again.

Use a clean brush. That doesn't mean it has to be expensive. A flat varnish brush is best. (See Buying Supplies.) To keep the brush clean between coats you should keep it in mineral spirits or turpentine. This will keep it clean and soft and ready for each new coat. What I do is to puncture the top of an olive jar (or similar container) and force the brush handle through the hole so that when the top is screwed back on the jar the brush hangs suspended in the solvent. The bristles should not touch the bottom of the jar or they will curl. When you don't plan to use your brush for a number of weeks, clean it and wrap it in cellophane wrap.

After you have applied your coat of varnish leave your

piece alone. Put it on a shelf where it cannot be disturbed. The less you fuss with it, the better finish you'll have.

The important part is the drying time. If you let the varnish dry a full twenty-four hours between coats, you can't miss. If you don't, you're dead. Or your project is. Sometimes the varnish can label says that the varnish will dry in a couple of hours. It will dry so you can touch it, but if you do the fingernail test, you will know that it isn't dry to a hard finish. Press your fingernail into the surface. If it leaves an indentation the varnish is not dry all the way through. When you apply another coat on top of the one that was not completely dry, you form a soft build-up. With each new coat of varnish you are building up a soft finish that will ultimately begin to dry and pull away from the item causing the entire design to lift off. If you sand this soft finish, it will gum up or pull and it will be impossible to create the kind of finish so beautiful in decoupage.

After your varnish is thoroughly dry apply two more coats the same way before sanding. When the third coat is dry you can begin to sand between coats of varnish. Using "Wet-ordry" super-fine sandpaper (wet very, very slightly), sand with a very light hand. Do not bear down. You aren't trying to sand off the finish. You just want to smooth out any particles that have dried on the varnish. Each time your varnishing coat is completely dry you sand it this way. Don't forget to wipe off the sand grit after each sanding.

The number of coats of varnish is up to you. I like a slightly raised effect so that I can feel the design. This is achieved by stopping the varnished coats before the design is totally submerged. So how many coats of varnish to use is determined when you get there. If your design is almost completely submerged and you've decided it has enough, or *you've* had enough, stop. If you intend to antique, don't sand the last coat of varnish. I'll tell you why when we get to antiquing, but for now, just DON'T.

If you are not planning to antique your item, then you should do a final sanding now. I have another little trick to achieve a smooth finish. Mix up some soapsuds in a cup with more soap than water. Swish your sandpaper around in it and for your final sanding, sand your decoupaged item getting it good and wet and soapy. Wipe off everything with a rag when you're done. Using a #oooo steel wool, go over the whole item again. This should give you an extra fine finish. If you do antique, come back to these steps for the

final finish after you have antiqued and varnished again.
Now apply a coat of paste wax exactly as directed on the
can—rub and buff it so that it glows with the fine patina of
beautiful furniture. And that's it. Your piece is completed.

Antiquing: you're not getting older, just better

Overnight aging via antiquing is one of the best ways I
know to give your decoupaged piece character. Unfortunately, most antiquing is poorly done. This is an art and
should be done carefully with an understanding of the process and why it's being done. The basic antiquing mixture
that I use is an earth-color, raw umber base the formula for
which is given on page 36. There are also premixed solutions
that you can use. Whichever you use, the procedure is the
same.

What is antiquing? When something is old—really old, not
just fake old— it has age marks. Most of the time it is worn
down in spots where it has been handled most. There are
dirty areas where dirt has collected over the years and become part of the piece. The poor antiquing jobs that I've
seen were done poorly because of a misunderstanding of
what antiquing represents. It is not dirty brush strokes.
Nothing is uglier than dark brush strokes across a piece
masquerading as antiquing. Yuck! Long ago I did it too,
so you're not the only one. I guess anybody who bought an
antiquing kit when they were first popular did it that way.
But give it some thought. If a piece has been sitting in someone's attic for a hundred years, it has accumulated some
dirt to say nothing of the use and abuse it received when it
was used. So before beginning, let's play a little game. Pre-
tend that your item has been constantly in use. Put it down
and then go to it and touch it where it seems most natural.
For instance, if it is a box, open it. Notice where your hands
touch it. Now move it to another location. Where do your
fingers touch it when lifting it? These are the areas that
would get the most use and would therefore show dirt and
wear the most. If your box has a clasp in front, dirt would
collect around the clasp as well as around the hinges on the
back. The corners, since they protrude, would get banged

most and would catch dirt. "Dirt" is what I call the aging or antiquing. If your design is slightly raised, "dirt" would naturally collect around the design. When antiquing is applied in a very subtle way around the designs, it emphasizes and gives character that is barely perceptible, almost like a smoky outline.

Once you understand where to apply the antiquing it is equally important to know how to do it. I can't emphasize this enough—lightly! For a small object, use a flat varnish brush (no more than a quarter inch) and brush the antiquing over a portion of the object. With a clean rag begin to rub it off. Wipe off much of the excess with one or two swoops across. Then go back and with the brush begin to push the antiquing into the corners and crevices of the design. The antiquing should never go across the design when it is finally finished. The design should be in the clear with the "dirt" left around it—but hardly noticeable. Leave small deposits in corners and around hinges, but not in clear parts. Where the item is painted and varnished but has no design covering it, there should be hardly any antiquing. Keep wiping and pushing the antiquing around until it is only faintly there. It takes some practice to learn the art of antiquing, but after a few pieces you'll have the hang of it.

Once I had a lovely elderly lady in my class. When I explained how to antique she asked if this was necessary. I told her that it wasn't, but it adds such a nice subtle touch as well as covering up a mistake or two. "Well," she said, "I'm in my eighties and everything I have is old. I'm at a point where I want everything to look fresh and new."

Now about covering up those mistakes. Of course your objective is to have everything you make come out perfect, but by the time you are ready to antique you will have spent quite a lot of time on an item, and it would be a shame to throw it out just because there is a brush hair stuck in the varnish or a scratch on the very top. Antiquing goes a long way toward covering up or at least fooling the eye. If your piece originally had scratch or gouge marks, you're lucky. They can add interest, and when antiquing is added to those places it will sink in and look quite natural. If your varnish has chipped because you dropped it before it was dry, add a spot of antique mix here and it will just look like an age spot. Perhaps you put the hinges on crooked. You can add a bit more antiquing around the hinges to make them look as though they are straight, or at least straighter. If you have a drip mark from your paint or varnish that was not sanded smoothly enough, camouflage it with a little antiquing. If some particles dried on your finish leaving you with an all-but-perfect surface, the antiquing will help it to look better.

I mentioned earlier that you should not sand your last coat of varnish before applying the antiquing. This is very important. Let me explain why. If you are familiar with the art of scrimshaw, you will understand. This is the art of etching on ivory, traditionally on whales' teeth, and was first done by sailors during long months at sea. The tooth was sanded smooth and then a design or drawing was etched, or scratched, into the surface. A substance much like black ink was then rubbed over the surface and wiped off again. The black remained where the drawing lines were etched into the tooth. When you sand your decoupaged item you form scratch marks that you can hardly see because you are sanding over many coats of varnish. If you then apply your antiquing mixture over the sanded surface, when you wipe it away it will remain in the scratch marks and there will be a crisscross of black (or antiqued) lines across your decoupage. These are hard to ignore, and I would say if this happens the piece is ruined—there is nothing you can do to undo this situation.

If you find the antiquing mixture begins to dry before you have completed the job, add a little mineral spirits to a cloth and wipe it off. Then start again or continue. If you are using an all-purpose antiquing mix, read the label. I think you can just use water to wipe it off.

Antiquing set dries in about an hour, but it is best to leave it alone for a day. This is because it has an oil base. It is absolutely necessary that antiquing be dry—if it is still wet when you apply your final coat of varnish, it will be smeared. When the antiqued piece is completely dry apply a coat of varnish over the antiquing to protect it. After this is dry you can sand and do the final steps, explained on page 70.

What you cut is what you get

A delicate piece

Today I cut up a pumpkin. Two years ago I began cutting what I consider the biggest cutting challenge ever encountered. It is an eerie, beautifully interesting print. If cut a little at a time using very sharp scissors, you can cut almost anything.

About three years ago I acquired a beautiful round box that had been made in Sweden. It was originally made as a bread box, but these lovely boxes have since been used to hold yarn for needlework or knitting and are often lined with exquisite fabric. The white wood is so elegant that it should not be covered with paint. However, this particular box had been wrapped in pink tissue paper which had gotten wet. When unwrapped, the wood had streaks of pink over the top. Not much good as is. That was a few years ago, and I have made several attempts to decoupage it since. This box is quite special and unusual in size and shape, and every time I began to work on it I would stop. I couldn't seem to find the perfect design for this project.

At the end of the summer we loaded the car with all our belongings and the box that had been previously left behind. This was it. I decided it would be now or never.

While searching for our Halloween pumpkin it suddenly occurred to me. The shape of the box was just right. Now where was that print I had started cutting a few summers back? Jon says you can't open a book in our house without tiny cutout designs falling from the pages. I have a perfectly delightful old chest with thin drawers that are just right

for holding cutouts, but they always get left between pages until I am ready for them. It didn't take long to locate the right book. There between the pages was my half cut up "pumpkin on the vine," a little crumpled but not beyond repair.

It's not really a beautiful print, but it's so interesting. When cutting something this intricate it is almost impossible to eliminate every single extra bit of white paper. I wish I could tell you that it is magnifying glass perfect, but it isn't. If you decide to tackle a project like this, you really should try to cut as well as possible or don't do it at all. Nothing looks worse than the white outline of a jagged cutting job.

There is more to a good design than composition, and this is cutting. If you have a beautiful intricate design and can do a terrific cutting job, you will be able to create an unusual project. The ability to cut is perfected with practice, and this skill can open up an endless variety of possibilities.

A lacy design like this one takes time and patience and should not be tackled by a beginner.

Lots of glue should be applied directly to the box before laying down the pieces of a very delicate design. Applying glue to the box will allow you to move the design around until it is just right.

Be sure that each piece is thoroughly coated so that no detail will be missed. Each part must be securely in place.

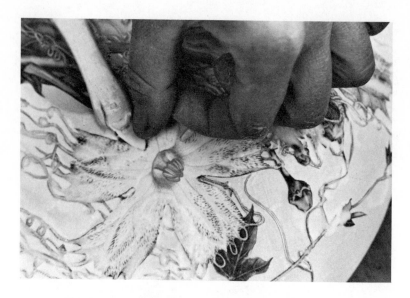

Sometimes a piece must be cut to fit. The design is fitted around the handle so that part of the cutout will extend up onto the handle to make it part of the overall design.

Part of the stem is cut so that the vines appear to be twining over and under the handle. This must be done so that it seems quite natural. If some pieces of stem are needed as extenders, they may be added from something else.

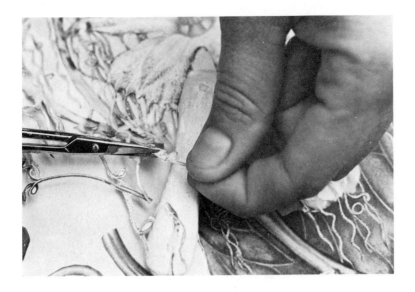

Snip little bits where it is not noticeable when you need extra pieces here and there. Whenever possible, it is best to use extra pieces from the print you are working on rather than from another source.

The curly vines of the pumpkin plant are the perfect detail for the handle. A tweezer is often used to pick up these tiny cutouts.

The pumpkin is fitted over the curve of the box lid and is creased to fit. Press creases flat when this is necessary to make a design conform to a shape. When varnished it is smooth to the touch.

Since there are so many squiggly tendrils to this cutout design, I applied lots of glue over these areas to be sure that I didn't miss anything.

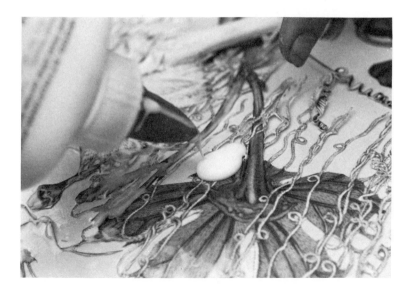

If there are air bubbles where there is not enough glue under the print, they will begin to lift the design after it is varnished.

When applying cutouts to a curved area take extra care to secure them. The excess glue can be removed once the design is in place. This is done with a damp sponge that is patted over the whole thing until there is no trace of glue on the surface of the box or top of the design.

Sometimes it is great fun to do something really complicated. The first thing you ever made was a plaque. Okay, you did that. No big deal. But the next time you should do something a bit more challenging. And before long you should be looking for prints that really boggle the imagination. The point is not to look for impossible things to cut, but to try new ideas. Take it a little at a time and you'll surprise yourself.

After several coats of varnish have been applied to the entire box you are ready to antique. With a large piece, work on a small area at a time. Smooth the antiquing mixture around with a varnish brush and then wipe most of it away with a clean cloth, leaving a trace of antiquing around the design but not streaked across the print. Spread some of the antiquing around raised areas such as handles, hinges, corners, or catches. This is where "dirt" might collect. Keep it subtle.

Cutting
tiny things

Lots of botanical prints that you find will have tiny buds or petals that are practically lost on the page. Often they are disregarded or cut away when cutting the larger designs. It is these tiny overlooked "specks" that are also a challenge to the advanced cutter. If they are used on a very tiny object, they become an important design. Aspirin tins make wonderful small gift ideas for pill boxes and can be designed with the leftovers. You'd be surprised how large an insignificant closed bud can become. If you paint the background a dark pastel, such as soft green or burnt orange, most otherwise insignificant designs will show up beautifully. The buds I've used are generally pale in color, like white or pale pink. They are almost indiscernible on a page. When arranged on a dark background you can't believe how they come alive. They are really fun to cut, but again, sharp scissors and good lighting is required. An around-the-neck magnifying glass may be helpful here also. Never waste any of those cutouts. What you don't need today may be just what you want tomorrow.

An aspirin tin.

New ideas for outdoor projects

Address oval

This form of identifying and personalizing a home has been a favorite of mine for years. An address oval can have a name or numbers on it. One of my students made four—one for each season. Isn't that a great idea? Some people prefer an overall design where the designs and numbers are combined into a flowing pattern. Other plaques can be designed with the numbers as the focal point. Using the oval shape, the design should follow these lines and act as an accent for the numbers. Thus, the size of the numbers or letters becomes an important design factor. They shouldn't be too small to read. At the same time if they are too large, they will dominate and leave room for little else.

One of the very first ovals I did was a numeral 3 for my friend Joan Clifford in Nantucket. I used my usual satiny indoor wood varnish. It just so happens that this house is one of the older homes on a historic street and one of the points of interest for the Nantucket tour bus. Needless to say, the address oval got a lot of exposure and comments. However, the Nantucket weather does terrible things to wood. The oval got as much weather exposure as people exposure. So over the past few years the sun, moisture, and salt air began to have its effects on the varnish. It began to crack and pull away from the surface, causing peeling. How could I have the tour bus pointing out this lovely home with the chipped and peeling address oval? I called Joan and told her that my work was guaranteed for life and that next summer she'd have a new oval.

The door is Shaker blue so I used blue and purple thistle flowers which grow wild in Nantucket. The background color is ivory. The thistle print appeared to be a bit stiff for the oval shape, but since I liked the design and felt it appropriate for this project, I decided to use it anyway.

First I cut it out using very sharp cuticle scissors. I did a little at a time which is a good idea when working on such a detailed print. This way you will be fresh each time you pick it up and the cutting will be consistent. After it was all cut out, I cut the thistle apart at various points. Then I began arranging it in as many different ways as possible. Impossible! It just wouldn't work. I put it aside several times. Though it is important to stick with a project long enough to make it work, that's easier said than done.

Of course it's simpler to use a print and object that design well together right off, but now and then a challenge is fun. When you have pieced a design together in a layout remove each piece as you work with it. This way you will know exactly where to place it. This is sometimes difficult with a three-dimensional object, but quite simple with a plaque. When working with fragile pieces wet your fingers before spreading the glue. You may want to dilute the glue slightly

Often a design does not seem just right for the shape of an object. It can, however, be adjusted and made to fit by cutting it into pieces.

Once the design is cut apart where it seems most natural the pieces can be arranged and rearranged until the best pattern is achieved.

If a stem or branch is a bit stiff and you want it to curve around the shape you are working on, you can mold it slightly when it is wet with glue.

After several coats of
varnish the antiquing is
brushed over the entire
oval.

Avoid getting fingerprints
on the piece as you work.
Wipe off most of the
antiquing leaving only
traces. The antiquing will
slide nicely over the
varnished surface.

Push the antiquing in
around the design but not
covering it. The antiquing
adds character and should
leave only a hint of an
outline to accent the
design.

When holding the plaque place a finger on a part of the design where there is no antiquing to avoid fingerprints.

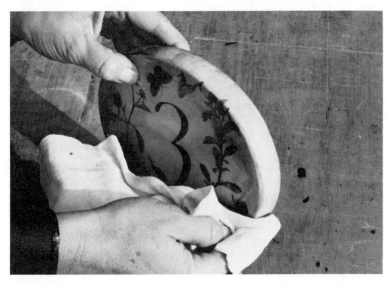

The antiquing should extend around the outer edges as well as the back so that it is completely uniform. Check for fingerprints so that you can wipe them away when finished. Set aside to dry.

The antiquing used is dark brown earth color and should be applied with a very light hand. When dry this is protected with another coat of varnish.

with a drop of water. Spread the glue evenly on the back of your design. Carefully lift one edge and peel the piece off the table. Gently hold the loose end and set it in place on the oval. If the stem or branch is a bit stiff, you can mold it slightly when it is wet with glue. By stiff I mean that it goes straight when you want to curve it around the shape you are working on. Stiff branches can often be made to curve if you do it quickly and carefully so the stem doesn't tear. Once it is pressed down in position you cannot remove it. Be sure to clean off your fingers before gluing and placing the next piece. When working with fragile stems they often get stuck to your fingers and rip apart if you haven't cleaned your hands first. One by one you glue each cutout in place forming your finished project.

When doing a plaque overlap some of the designs onto the sides. Now go over each cutout with your clean damp sponge. With your brush handle roll over each cutout to be sure all air bubbles are squeezed out and excess glue removed.

Since this oval will be used outdoors, like the previous one, the finish must be harder than the one I used before, which was an indoor wood varnish. This time I decided to use a polyurethane finish—which is a plastic finish that is often used on floors. It creates a very hard surface and comes in a glossy or satin finish. While varnish creates a finer looking surface and has a certain glow you don't get from poly-urethane, it is not as tough. It is difficult to sand poly-urethane to a smooth surface because of its toughness, and for small indoor projects varnish is best.

Spar or deck varnish which is used on boats could also be used for the address oval, but polyurethane is best. However, it does cost more than varnish and it has a stronger odor. It takes a little longer to dry, but it dries clearer than varnish. Use good ventilation when applying this stuff because it may make your eyes sting.

Judy and Joel's jeep

Often an inspiration for a decoupage project comes in strange forms. Friends on Nantucket decided to buy a jeep which soon became an island joke because it kept every me-chanic on Nantucket steadily employed all summer. It got so that nobody would get in the thing for fear of his life, and you could hear it bucking down the street from half a mile away. Needless to say, this was not a new jeep, but "a real good buy."

One evening Judy went to pick up Joel at the airport. The airport is at least three miles from town and when she got there she discovered the drive shift would only work in reverse. When Joel climbed into the jeep for the trip home, Judy quite naturally put the thing in reverse and backed into town.

By the end of the summer the jeep had a permanent spot reserved at the curb's edge and Judy drove a rented car. We all agreed that the jeep had character and didn't deserve to simply die, so mutual friends agreed to fix it up over the winter and use it. It was also only fitting to do something appropriate to spruce up the outside. You guessed it. A decoupaged jeep. Why not? Do you think there are many?

Actually, the process was the same as for any outdoor decoupage project. So if you are planning to do a front door or a mailbox, the procedure is similar.

It was easier to decide to do this particular project than it was to decide what to do with it and how to do it. I mean, what in the world do you put on a jeep? Another concern was the weather since we had to be sure that the temperature would be warm and that there would be clear skies for at least a week while we worked.

I finally decided a "campy" or off-beat look was what was needed. Since the friends who would be using the jeep have a sailboat rental business, we all thought it would be appropriate to design a seal for the door that could advertise the business. I began looking for ideas. First I checked books, then local souvenir stores. Mostly what I found were prints and books of sailboats. I felt this would be too ordinary, and besides, have you ever tried to cut out a sailboat? Too many crisscrossing lines. Finally, I found something that I had never used before and would not have guessed would work for decoupage. A coloring book. This one had pictures of crazy boats from long ago. The paper is so dreadful that I would never recommend it unless you just have to have a design that can only be found in a coloring book. The paper is like toilet paper; not quite as bad, but almost. More like construction paper, only not as good. It is so absorbent that it does not hold up under the varnish. Also, coloring it presents another hurdle. As I said a challenge can sometimes be fun. Or at least challenging.

I tried different methods of coloring the designs and finally used Magic Markers because I liked the effect better than paint or colored pencils. Practicing on pictures I didn't want to use, I decided that the markers would work just fine. I also tried the varnish over the markers and the color didn't run as I expected, but the page became totally transparent. All the print showed through. Spraying the picture first with Krylon didn't help at all. Next I tried pasting the print on plain white paper. I varnished again. The print still showed through. This was all done on the pictures that I would not be using, since I was still experimenting. Then I decided maybe black was the thing, so I painted the back with black tempera paint. This worked although the colors on the front became duller. But I felt that I could live with this.

The back of the coloring book page was coated with black tempera paint so that the print would not show through.

This design reminded us of an emblem, which is why we thought it would look quite nice on the door of the jeep.

One of the designs I chose looked just like an emblem. It was a Viking ship within a circular outline, and there were grapes hanging down into the ship as well as some other silly things. I felt it could look quite nice on the door, and it seemed just the right size as well. Jon is better at coloring than I am (it must be his graphic design background), so he did the honors. First he painted the background with a very pale blue watercolor paint. Then the grapes were done with pink and purple marker. The fish were blue, purple, and green, the sail orange with pink trim, the boat shocking pink, the sailor orange with a red beard, green for the grape stems, and a black border. We wanted to be sure that you could see the emblem from far away, so subtlety wasn't what we were after. When it was done the back was painted black and when dry the picture

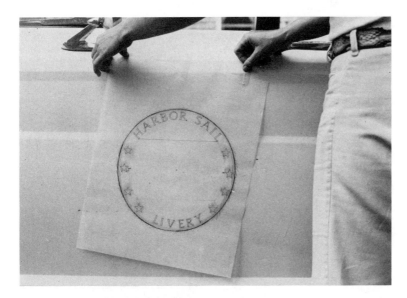

The border design and firm's name were first done on tracing paper to use as an outline.

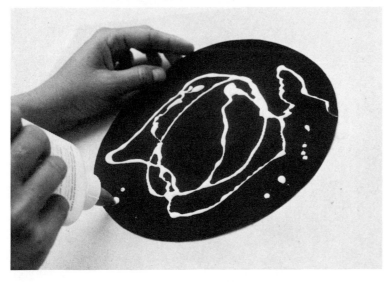

Glue was applied to the back of the emblem design and spread evenly to the outer edges before design was glued to jeep.

was cut out. (Additionally, painting the back made the design stiff and easier to work with.) We decided to have a border around the outside of the design with the name of the business within the border. This also enlarged the design, which by itself was a little smaller than I wanted it to be. For this Jon drew the border, the border design, and placed the firm's name, all on a separate piece of tracing paper. To make the letters for the name, we used Letraset Transfer Type. After all, how many people can draw perfect letters? Letraset is available in art supply stores in any kind of type you want. Each sheet has several of each letter in both upper and lower case, and you simply line up each letter, one at a time, and rub it off onto the surface you are working on.

In order to center the design in the middle of the door, I taped the tracing from the top so that it could hang

Positioning the design on the door.

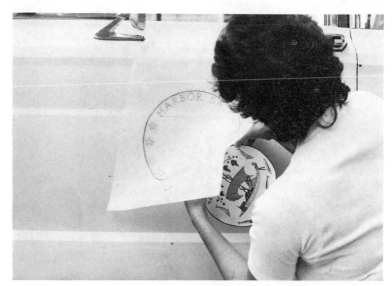

Transferring the letters.

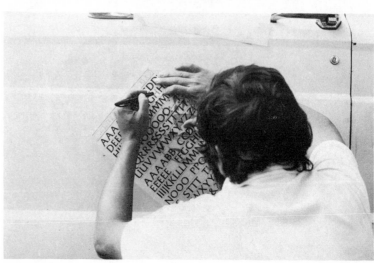

down onto the door. Then I lifted it up from the bottom and slid the design under it and using Elmer's glue, glued the design to the door. Since there was a ridge over the door right where the picture was placed, it had to be firmly pressed down so that it would fit neatly over this curve. Using the tracing paper on top of the design I smoothed it down with my hand so that I would not have to touch the picture and risk soiling it.

Then Jon began to apply the type. He knew exactly where to place each letter because he had previously made a tracing of the name to use as a guide. When the name "Harbor Sail Livery" was done he painted a circle around the outside with purple marker. Using black marker he added some stars. This was our undoing. When I applied the varnish the border design began to smear, run, drip, everything. Quickly I began to wipe away the mess. Rub-

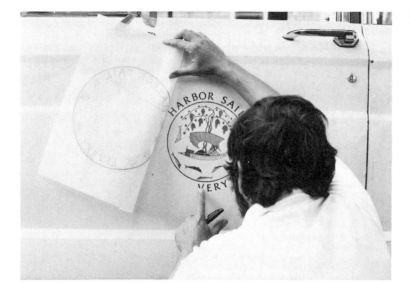

Press letters down firmly.

Stars and decorative border were added.

bing smeared it more, dulled the designs, but didn't remove it entirely. The only thing to do was to get rid of the outer rim and those stars. This had to be done without smearing the rest of the design. When it was patted dry we stood back to view the damage. Not good. But not irreparable. At this point, while it was still slightly damp, we removed any remaining varnish with turpentine.

We decided a pea-green paint would be a good color for a border, and why hadn't we thought of it before. I never liked those stars anyway! So using a ruler to steady his arm, Jon was once again nominated to paint the border. Acrylic paint this time, not a marker. Sometimes it pays to have an optimistic attitude. Actually, the green border did look better and gave the whole thing a more complete look. It was truly a customized emblem. After that I once again applied the varnish. Since it is an upright object

The Magic Marker used for the border smeared and ran when the varnish was applied.

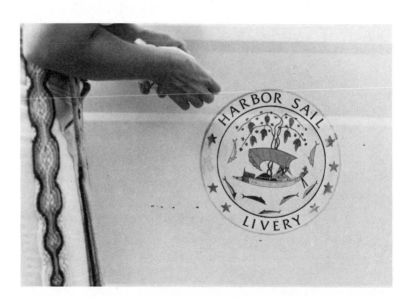

Jon applying green acrylic paint over the messed up border. A ruler is used to steady his arm in order to keep within the outline.

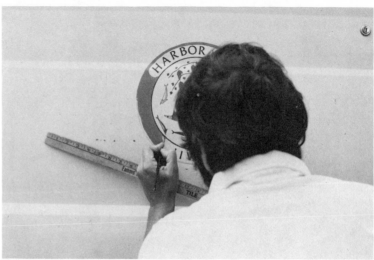

each coat had to be applied very carefully. A thin coat was applied each time and the entire door was covered so that the color would be even.

Since the night air is damp on the island, each coat was applied early in the morning to give it the entire day to dry in the sun. By evening the varnish was dry. I used an out-door varnish and applied ten coats with sanding between each of the last five.

What we discovered about our mistakes was that while we had tested the markers on paper that was absorbent, the metal of the jeep wouldn't take the color. It wouldn't dry. It was at this point that we were convinced it was a failure and Harbor Sail Livery might have to hang a towel out the window to cover the door lest they look like a slipshod outfit. After two coats of paint we couldn't even see the mistake showing through. So you see, even the so-called experts make mistakes that no amount of antiquing can cover up. I must add that when it finally came time to begin varnishing again Jon went inside not being able to watch—coward that he is.

That night our friends came to dinner and were surprised with the new sign. The only problem remaining was to get the jeep back to their house since it had no brakes and at this point wouldn't even go in reverse.

Now you know what I meant when I said that I was a trial-and-error craftsperson. While we had problems with the coloring-book designs, I would like to encourage you to be open-minded about sources for your design material. You can only learn the limitations of the craft by experimenting. It is in this way that you will also discover new ideas or techniques. Take risks. Often they lead to the unexpected which can be better than the known.

After two coats of paint the mistake underneath cannot be seen. Now the door is ready for several coats of varnish.

Decoupage on the high seas

Not one to be daunted by a near disaster, I refused to let a coloring book get the best of me. Besides, it seemed a good idea to carry this theme a bit further. One of the Harbor Sail Livery boats was to be our next outdoor project.

After much talk and many drawings and plans we narrowed down the possible designs for the boat. Designs can be "made" in various ways. It is not always necessary to arrange preprinted cutouts. This was to be a joint project with all our friends in on the act. It seemed logical to use another coloring-book design to match the jeep's—sort of a "corporate identity program." The major problem was to fight the temptation to go sailing so we could work on the boat before Labor Day.

You may wonder why in the world I would decide to

One of the Harbor Sail Livery boats might make a good outdoor project.

decoupage a boat. It's quite simple. I wanted to do something different. I wanted to do an outdoor project, and I wanted to show that decoupage can be tried on practically anything made of wood.

It was near the end of the summer and the weather had been so fabulous that we were almost praying for rain so that we could get some work done indoors. We spoke too soon. With only two weeks left until Labor Day we had to do the boat immediately or not at all. But it didn't look as though we would get the chance. Once the clouds came it seemed they'd never leave, and we couldn't take the chance of applying the varnish and then having it rain. Another factor was that the boat was on the sandy shore and the air had to be calm. If you think dust is a problem in the varnish, ponder the prospect of sand.

After five rainy days I couldn't believe it. Served me right for waiting all summer. How could this happen? In a flash the summer weather was gone. Every now and then there would be a splotch of sunshine, and Jon and I would race

This design was created from the coloring book used for the jeep in order to follow the theme.

down to the boatyard. I had already cut out the design that we had painted from the coloring book that we used for the jeep design. Having learned a lesson from the jeep, we only used run-proof oil colored pencils and painted the back black. The stern and bow of the boat are brick red, almost maroon, so the design had to be light. We tried it on every part of the boat. The design was a bit small for the size of the boat, but it is still nice. Jon lettered *Harbor Sail* on the Egyptian boat design. It really is a fun kind of thing. (You didn't think that I was really going to decoupage the entire boat did you? Maybe next year when we have more time.)

Well, we tried the design on different parts as well as on some of the other boats. I'm always a little nervous about imposing my designs on others. This is something I never do, so I was a bit apprehensive. Once we decided where it looked best, I applied the glue and on it went. Now after two experiences with this kind of paper I say, "Never, never

The cutout design is "tried on" for size and looks in various positions to see where it will show up best.

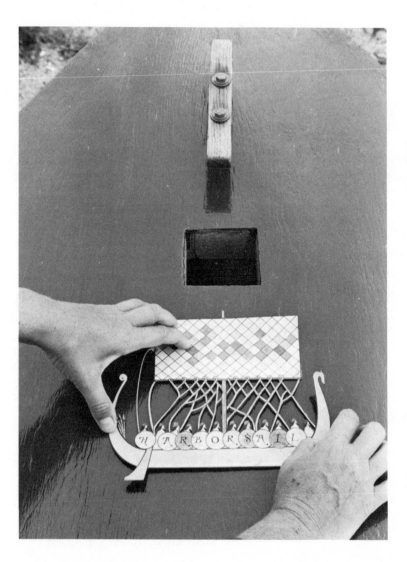

again." It is so awful. The color changes when the varnish is applied, the black on the back came through and it just wasn't fun to work with. I floated the varnish on the design to seal it because the drizzles were starting again and the sun had disappeared.

This project should have spar or deck varnish used on it to make it weatherproof. Spar varnish is never used for indoor furniture but is perfect for an outdoor project. Since this varnish never really dries clear through, it can expand and contract with the weather. This is necessary when working on an outdoor project that is wood. When doing decoupage on metal outdoors check the section on decoupaging metal objects.

By next summer Harbor Sail Livery should have their whole fleet with identifying symbols. In Nantucket you can now rent a sailboat that is probably one of the only decoupaged boats around.

This design is quite fragile and must be applied very carefully, taking care not to use too much glue since the paper is quite transparent.

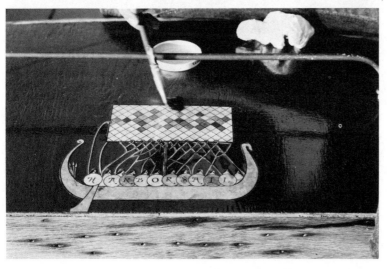

Varnish should be applied on a dry, clear day when doing an outdoor project. Each coat should be thoroughly dry before applying the next.

Inspiration for designs

What am I bid for this box of junk?

Have you ever been to an auction? Quite by accident I discovered that auctions are a great place to pick up things to decoupage. It's also a fun thing to do when the weather is nice.

On a recent trip through Connecticut I was overwhelmed by the skyrocketing prices in antique shops. A friend came

Handmade box by Gramp. Decoupaged with a Connecticut theme by Ruth Linsley.

to visit and brought with him a box filled with unusual and interesting one-of-a-kind oddities. He said he had purchased the box for fifty cents at an auction and had become an avid attender at local auctions. He told us that sometimes things are way overpriced, but often you can get a real buy. The following weekend it was sunny and warm for a November day, and we scanned the paper for an auction announcement. Now don't misunderstand. It's not that we're easily led, but we can't resist the thought of a bargain. The one that looked the best was in a town that was over an hour's drive away, but we were game. I should have said an hour to find the town, but another hour to find the thirty-two room farmhouse where the auction was taking place. Now doesn't that sound exciting? You have to admit, you might even have gone yourself.

By the time we got there all the furniture was gone, but the barns were loaded with odds and ends. Mostly odds and ends that even the oddest wouldn't want. But we were there mainly to get the hang of it all.

Ideas can come in unexpected ways. On this trip we had to cross the Connecticut River from Rocky Hill to South Glastonbury by ferry. I've lived in Connecticut all my life and didn't know this little ferry existed. When we reached the other side we discovered a sign giving the ferry's history. On the sign was the Connecticut state seal, and right then I decided that a Connecticut box would be interesting. This gave me more ideas. How about a box or plaque for your state? It could have the state flower on it and other symbols representing what your state stands for. A historic landmark is often an interesting subject for decoupage. The inside of the box can then be lined with a map of the state.

Lined with a map of Connecticut.

What's your style?

Everyone has a style. When you're just starting out you are developing your skills in technique. At the same time, you are developing a style. What makes a design "work"? How does a designer create a style? If you were to do many decoupage pieces over and over, before long your things would begin to look similar in style. On the other hand, someone else would have created a different style. When you looked at the various pieces you could then tell which ones belonged to the different designers by their style. Each would reflect the person who did them. Many decisions go into making up that style. First you decide the size of the

project, then the color, shape, and finally the subject. Everybody has to make the same general decisions, but each person will make them differently and that combination of decisions is what determines a style. Pablo Picasso was a versatile artist, sculptor, potter, muralist, etc., yet regardless of the medium, the style that is Picasso is obvious in all his works of art.

In developing a style, you are influenced by many things including the work of other craft designers. It's important to understand the value of the influence of fine work in your field. You have to be careful, however, because too strong an influence can lead to copying. If you copy the work you admire, you run the risk of being locked into somebody else's style.

Where do you find influences that you can relate to designing decoupage pieces? All around you. Everything that you see influences the choices that you eventually make in developing your style. You have to develop the ability not only to be aware of things that intrigue you, but also to relate them to the decoupage project you are working on. Have you ever noticed signs? Not just street signs such as "Go Slow" or "Stop," but the signs over stores—signs announcing promises of what you can expect to find within, some with great personality and some well designed but completely meaningless. They can be an inspiration for your own designs. When we first became aware of signs and started photographing them I quickly realized how they could be an interesting subject for decoupage. Doesn't the round sign for the Nantucket Institution for Savings Bank remind you of the emblem that we did for the jeep?

When we were in West Stockbridge, Massachusetts, we suddenly noticed that every store had a special sign perfectly designed for the place of business within. Obviously, an artist had come to town. In some cases the signs outdid the business. When I saw the Wood Spirit sign I decided that I had to find a print of an old knarled tree. Wouldn't it be delightful in an entrance hallway? The trunk could start at the front door right on the floor and the branches could spread out in different directions leading off into the rooms beyond. With many coats of polyurethane it could be walked over without any harm coming to the design. I haven't found that tree yet, but I'm looking. If not on a floor, it might be easier to stick with a small box. The tree shouldn't be too hard to find in a smaller scale. Then other things could be added to the scene. A bird in the tree. A cutout photograph of a small child sitting under the tree might be done for a personalized gift.

The bookstore sign shows a rising sun. This is always a good symbol to use for decoupage and not too difficult to find. If you like it and can't find a sun as nicely designed, it isn't too difficult to make it yourself. The graphic design could be cut from paper in the exact colors that you like. This could be a great design for a small box especially if it covers the box entirely.

The lettering is also of interest. Have you thought about using a saying for your decoupage? How about a decoupage greeting card? The lettering can go right over the design or it can go on a plaque with the decoupage designs around it. We wondered if the sign designer had limited his talents to West Stockbridge or was on the move, beautifying all of New England's tiny villages.

Closer to home we found more unusual signs. Designs don't have to be realistic. Graphic design can sometimes work for a decoupage project. Although it isn't the traditional design we usually think of in decoupage, a good design can be interesting no matter where it's found. Old church windows are often inspiring. Stained glass windows have fabulous shapes and may spark an idea. Art deco and art nouveau books are a good place to start if you are interested in finding some unusual ideas. You might use this style for an overall pattern. There are paperback books that are inexpensive and have beautiful and subtle designs in fabulous pastel colors. These are interesting departures from the type of designs usually associated with decoupage.

Design
subtleties

Decoupage does not have to dominate your decorating scheme; in fact, no single piece should scream out for attention. The nicest thing about decoupage is that it is easy to live with. The traditional aspects of this craft make most pieces at home in any room and in any type of home. Often you can use several pieces in a room if you are careful with your choice of design and color.

The candlesticks are a good example of this. The background of the short candlesticks is sand color with an accent of pastel green on the top. The design uses pale green stems with the tiniest drop of a faint pink bud. I use brown candles in these sticks. Completing this setting could be a set of decoupaged napkin rings. Rather than painting these rings, a dark walnut stain was used. Since the napkins are beige, a contrasting color of burnt or antiqued orange is used on the inside and outer top rim of each ring. For the Christmas holiday season, you might make white napkin rings decorated with red and green holly berries and leaves.

The dried flowers in a brown basket complete the subtle color scheme; holly leaves as a centerpiece are more appropriate for Christmas time. For springtime I use candlesticks with a white background and a yellow buttercup design. The napkin rings carry out this theme with white on the outside and yellow inside. More yellow flowers with green stems and leaves extend the springtime feeling; the centerpiece can be springtime flowers.

A fall theme is used on these walnut-stained napkin rings.

Subtle designs used on candlesticks can represent different seasons.

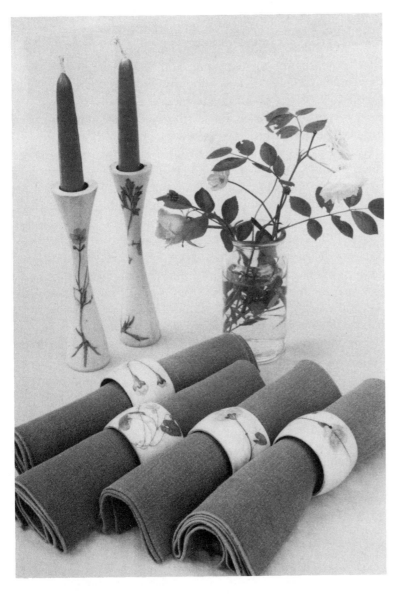

White candlesticks and napkin rings are decorated with yellow buttercups for a springtime setting. The insides of the napkin rings are painted yellow.

Decoupage on furniture

When I was about fifteen years old I had a passion to become a famous actress. Not an unusual ambition for a fifteen-year-old. I saw a play, *The Corn Is Green,* with Eva Le Gallienne on television and was prompted to write to her. In that letter I poured my heart's desires out and asked for advice about what to do. I received what was then my most treasured possession, a five-page handwritten letter. The letter has long since disappeared, something I shall never forgive myself for, but I will always remember the opening line. It read "Dear Leslie, I received your letter about wanting to become an actress. Must you?"

Obviously, the answer became clear enough. I mustn't. Well before you start to do decoupage on furniture ask yourself that basic question, must you? If you must, okay, but give it a bit of thought before you start. Have you had enough experience for such an undertaking? Are you ready to cope with the problems that were tiny on a trinket box but can be almost insurmountable on a dresser? If you've done a few projects and you want to try, then you are in for a rare treat. Making a box suddenly becomes child's play. If you thought it was exciting seeing a box develop, wait until you are up to your knees in furniture projects. The designing is a little scarier but the rewards are greater. And, of course, there will be no mistaking the fact that a decoupage piece is in the room. You will have to decide what it will be and where it will go and be darn sure that it will fit into the room. A box can be shoved around and placed almost anywhere; a piece of furniture is much more conspicuous.

This winter I did three furniture projects.

Walnut stain is applied to an unpainted dresser.

An undressed dresser

The first project was an unfinished dresser. What's the best way to approach a dresser? Since I have primarily worked with small items and cut small lacy designs, I had to readjust my thinking to bigness. Since I had begun with boxes, you might say I've been boxed in for some years.

It's exciting to face a new design problem on an item this size. You can see the whole thing take shape on a large scale. If you make any mistakes, it's also more apparent, but it's best not to think about that.

I had always wanted to do an unfinished piece of furniture, but it took me a long time to get around to doing it.

Once the stain is applied the excess is rubbed off with a clean cloth and the piece is left to dry overnight.

An attractive three-paneled wood screen for a desk top.

An old-fashioned child's desk and chair brought up-to-date with paint and decoupage.

*Little wood trinket
boxes are excellent for
a first project.*

This decoupaged design was inspired by the Old Mill in Nantucket, Massachusetts.

A lacy print makes an interesting cutting project and a unique design for this Swedish breadbox.

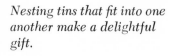
(Right) An unfinished dresser is stained and then decorated with a modern poster.

Nesting tins that fit into one another make a delightful gift.

These easily available film cans are decorated with tiny designs from magazines.

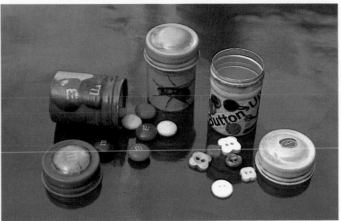

Aspirin tins are designed with little buds left over from other projects.

(Right) A decoupaged
director's chair is a
delightful addition to any
patio.

This director's chair has
decoupaged vines climbing
around legs and arms and
onto the canvas.

A parson's table is designed
with a Henri Rousseau
poster.

An address oval can
personalize your front door.

Handmade box by Gramp,
decoupaged by Leslie.

One of the reasons these pieces make such good decoupage projects is that they are readily available. If there isn't a raw furniture store in your area, this type of furniture is often sold through the mail. There is a wide variety to choose from, depending on your needs, and they are relatively inexpensive. There is no finish to contend with, as there is with a used piece, where you must deal with the old finish before applying a new one. All in all, raw furniture is a good bet. They are not made super well, but the sturdiness can be improved with glue here and there.

As is typical with these pieces, the dresser was rough to the touch and needed a good overall sanding job. Use a heavy-grade grit for this first sanding. If you have a sanding block, it makes the sanding of the large areas easier. You can also simply wrap the sandpaper around a flat piece of

Posters are an excellent source for material to use on large objects such as furniture.

wood of the size that feels comfortable to your hand. This contributes in a small way to saving sandpaper hands and manicured nails. Of course, you must get in there with sandpaper by hand for the areas between the drawers and any rounded sections. Wipe the sand dust off the entire dresser.

I had decided that this piece should be stained with a walnut color stain rather than painted. If you choose to paint, you would first apply a primer coat, available in hardware and paint stores.

It is much easier to stain than paint. Using a polyfoam brush simply smear the stain over every exposed part of the furniture. It is best to brush in one direction. The stain I like best is Minwax, and a small can goes a long way. You can pick the exact color you want from samples in the store. Usually stores that carry the raw furniture also sell the stain.

Once the stain has been applied, wait fifteen minutes and rub it off with a clean rag. Then allow it to dry overnight. If you decide to make it darker, you can apply another coat of stain the next day. I used only one coat. Remember, it will look a bit flat and dull when first stained, but as you apply coat after coat of varnish the color becomes rich and lustrous. The grain of the wood shows up, and a really crumby piece of furniture looks like dynamite. When the stain is completely dry the piece should be lightly sanded.

Try different posters before making a final selection.

Posters for design

You obviously can't use tiny prints that you cut from a book for a large piece. Large prints can be found in print and antique shops, but they are expensive and it isn't always easy to find exactly what you want. Posters can be just the thing to use for large projects for they are easily available at reasonable prices. I wanted the dresser to have a young feeling, and since the background would be a walnut brown, I thought that a poster design with reddish brown colors would be perfect. I had a poster that I was saving to use on something, and this turned out to be it. It was a picture of a girl with lots of trailing hair, riding on a bicycle. The colors were soft browns with bright yellow for accent.

Just to plunk the poster on the dresser would never do. It wouldn't fit first of all, and secondly, it would not look designed for the object. Also, it was too narrow for the width of the piece and had a border around it. It would have to be cut apart at various strategic places and made to look as if it were designed for this object.

First the knobs of the dresser were removed. This is easily done by unscrewing them from inside the drawers with a screw driver. After that I held the poster up to the dresser so that I could see it all different ways. My first thought was to place the design in such a way that I could put the knobs back when the design was done and not have them come out in awkward places. I soon discovered that however I placed the poster, the knobs ruined it. How could

A poster should be cut apart at various places so that it will fit as if designed for the object.

the girl have a knob coming out of her cheek? Or through her neck? It just wouldn't do. So I decided to sacrifice convenience for art's sake. The drawers would have to be pulled out from the sides. This is a problem to think about before selecting a design. Perhaps you can do better than I did.

Once you've decided how to go with the design, plunge in. This is where we separate the weak from the strong. If you ever thought you would become anxious about this craft, now's the time to bow out. But then again if you've come along this far, what have you got to lose? Just to be sure before I cut into the poster, I tried another one that I had. I held it up to the dresser to see if the design and color worked better. It didn't, so I felt more confident about forging ahead with my original plan. I studied the poster and decided to cut away as much of the surrounding area as I could without having it look strange. I wanted the girl's hair to flow across the drawers freely. I also didn't want the design to look like a poster, so I cut off the border and tried to cut away some of the paper around the flowers to make an uneven border. The advertisement at the bottom, "American Crescent Cycles" was also removed. This left an empty square that had to be dealt with later. The trees and bushes in the background and a crescent-shaped sun were interesting, so I wanted to keep them. I planned the design to start from the top of the dresser and continue down across each drawer. As you work on something that

Make a crease over the edge before cutting this piece away from the rest of the poster.

When cutting, leave enough of the design so that the edge can be glued under the top to eliminate any uneven cutting lines.

is not a flat surface, such as this, you have to compensate for the curves. Each piece has to be cut away from the whole while you are working on it. Then the next piece must be placed into position so that there is no break in the design. I first decided that each piece had to be glued so that it not only went over each curve but tucked under so that you couldn't see where it had been cut. This would make the design continuous.

After making a crease in the paper over the lower edge of the top of the bureau, I cut the piece away from the rest of the poster leaving enough of the design to glue under the top. I then applied the glue to this one strip of design and lay it carefully down in the exact position on the dresser. I used a rubber brayer, which is a roller, to smooth out the design. Using a large poster is tricky and you must be extra careful of air bubbles, so be sure that there is enough glue on the back and that all surfaces are firmly smoothed out. I'm not particularly crazy about using a brayer. I don't think that you get enough weight on the object. I really prefer the handle of the paint brush because it is made of wood and is stronger. A rolling pin is also good for this purpose. Keep a clean, damp sponge handy.

When you have done the first strip you are on your way. The reason that it's so important to do a perfect job on the first piece is that if it isn't placed on straight, when you line up successive pieces they will not all match. If the first piece is crooked, every drawer after that will be

When this strip of the poster is glued in place use a rubber brayer to smooth out the design. Be sure all air bubbles are pressed down firmly.

After the top part is securely glued down add glue to the strip that will be tucked under the top edge.

slightly off center. The entire design will be lopsided. I hope this is clear. It's a little bit hard to explain. Taking the rest of the poster, hold it up to the first part that is already on the dresser. A tiny strip must be cut to fit between the dresser drawer and the top. If you look at a dresser you will see that the drawers don't line up flush with one another. There is a thin space on the dresser itself that shows between each drawer. The design must cover this space also, or else you will have blank spaces between the designs on the drawers. Don't take the drawers out to work on this part. It is best to see it exactly the way it will look. Pull the drawers out a little so that you can fit the design in. It should extend a tiny bit behind each drawer. Using a screw driver or butter knife you can smooth this thin strip down making sure it lines up with the piece above it.

As you go along it gets easier, and it is a real joy to see it turning out. With the big pieces on each drawer be especially careful to smooth them down. Apply plenty of glue to each piece and take your time placing them so that every thing lines up. It takes awhile and shouldn't be hurried.

When I got to the bottom there I was left with the empty space on the right. With a poster you will usually find there is more design than you really need. If you are clever, you can cut some parts away so that it looks perfectly natural. I did this with some flowers from the side and the bottom. I now held them up to the empty space. They were fine except that they still weren't enough. What I needed was a bunch of flowers that could be growing from the

A strip of the design should be cut to fit in the space between the drawers so that there will not be blank spaces.

Using a screw driver, you can smooth this thin strip down making sure that it lines up with the piece above it.

bottom right up over the girl's skirt. What I had left was a chopped off skirt and half a bicycle tire.

When you need more prints to complete a design it is not a good idea to take something from another source. The style is completely different, the colors aren't the same, and the weight of the paper will be different. The best thing would have been to buy another poster. But this seemed silly for only one or two flowers, and besides I was working at night on this and I didn't have the time to run out looking for another exact poster. So I decided to use the word "Cycles" from the part that I had cut off. Along with the extra flowers that I did have, the whole space filled in very nicely. To finish the design, I added one green petal with a dew drop on it at the bottom hanging onto the base of the dresser. This was an unused leaf that I had previously cut away. You see, never throw anything away.

If I had bought another poster, I would have added some flowers to the sides to make this project flow together. I like the sides to be part of the whole, but there just wasn't enough to use.

Polyurethane in a semi-gloss finish was then used over the entire piece. This will give your piece of furniture a tough, strong protective coating as well as a lustrous glow. Each coat of finish should be applied at the end of the day so that it can dry overnight. As I have mentioned before, polyurethane is a plastic resin and is quite impervious to everything. It has a terrifically strong odor, however, and must be applied with good ventilation or you will get a

Press this piece down while wiping away excess glue with a damp sponge.

Be sure that each large piece lines up with the piece above it before cutting. Leave a little extra to tuck under the drawer.

Add glue to one part at a time when applying large pieces to dresser.

Smooth piece with a sponge to remove excess glue.

Cut excess pieces away after gluing.

A brayer like the one on the table is useful for smoothing out bubbles under large pieces glued on each drawer.

Extra odds and ends are added at the bottom to finish off the design.

Part of the advertisement is removed and "Cycles" is used to fill in space.

headache. It also has a tendency to make your eyes burn and become watery. I feel, however, that in spite of all these bothersome side effects it is worth using it to achieve a fine hard finish. This is why I recommend doing it at the end of the day. In this way the piece can dry undisturbed all night and you will not have to live with the smell during the day. It should be applied at room temperature.

I applied about six coats to the dresser which seemed to be sufficient. The finish dries very hard, and rather than sanding it between coats you should use a very fine steel wool, such as a ⚹oooo, which is usually found in hardware stores. Craft shops may have it, but I have not found it often here. The steel wool rub down will smooth the surface, but it must then be cleaned well with a rag so that there are no particles left to be trapped in the next coating.

The final application of polyurethane should be rubbed with steel wool and then waxed with a clear furniture paste wax. The stained piece of furniture will have a rich glow and actually look like fine wood.

This project can be a lot of fun and give you a great deal of satisfaction because you have something so beautiful and substantial when you are through. I think I enjoyed working on this better than most of my projects. But then, I say that every time I finish something new.

Dresser is finished with several coats of matte polyurethane.

My apologies to Henri Rousseau

Or if I may be so immodest, Leslie Linsley collaborates with Henri Rousseau. A small wood Parson's table is an excellent project for decoupage. You can buy them unfinished in any size, and they are easy to work on. You can design only the top or you can carry the design right down the legs as I did.

Originally, I was going to paint the table sand color, but the natural wood was so light that it wouldn't look as though it was painted. Also, I thought that a pale blue color was a good background for the dark green jungle scene I was contemplating using on the table. Blue is a color to be particularly careful with. Varnish has a slightly yellowing effect on a painted surface. It also darkens stained finishes by the way. When many coats of varnish are applied to a blue paint, the paint turns slightly green. Pink is another problem color. It turns a bit orangy. These are the only two that I have had difficulty with. I used a very pale blue. To achieve this color I used a very light sky-blue paint and added lots of white.

This Parson's table arrived without the legs attached. However, it is a simple task to screw the legs into place, if you use a hex wrench. If you don't have one they are available in any hardware store and come in all sizes. You must take the wood screw with you so that you're sure to get the right size. It is easiest to sand and paint the legs before attaching them to the base of the table.

Each leg is then held in position while you tighten the screws. Make sure that each screw is as tight as you can possibly make it so your table won't wobble. And that's it. Once assembled you're ready to begin.

The grain was quite rough on this unfinished piece and needed sanding with a heavy-grade paper before painting. If you sand well before painting, your paint job will be much better and won't require as much sanding after that. Because of the light color this table required three coats of paint. I was especially careful to do a good job on the legs since they would be exposed and most of the table top would be covered.

Once again posters can be a good design source for this type of project. I had decided to make this into a jungle scene, so I began looking around for ideas. I came upon

A wood Parson's table is an excellent decoupage project.

an offbeat jungle illustration by a French artist. It had the feeling that I wanted. However, the animals were really too large. The feeling needed for my imagined jungle scene was more on the order of a Henri Rousseau painting. Fortunately, I found just what I needed in poster form. Relatively speaking, posters are quite cheap. After all, where can you find large enough prints for around five dollars? I have been so excited about the possibilities that I want to decoupage everything in sight. You can be enormously creative with posters, and because they're so large they're easy to cut out.

This table is easy to assemble. Sand and paint before attaching legs.

Well, as you can see the poster and the table are a bit different in size. Originally this was to be a simple poster-glued-to-the-table-top sort of project, but I have a tendency to get carried away. The first thing that happens when faced with a large print that must be cut up is that an uneasy feeling starts to grow in the pit of your stomach and can only be described as terror. I hung the poster in the studio for a few days and now and then I'd get an idea. This is a good way to begin formulating a design. If you hang your print up you can live with it for a while before actually using it. That way you can come up with ideas, toss them around in your mind until you come up with one you're sure of. I'm always convinced that once I cut the print one way, I'll wish I'd planned it another. But then, of course, it's good to feel that each new project will be better than the one before.

There is just so long you can look at the overall print, and there's just so long you can plan. At some point you've

This Henri Rousseau poster will be cut to fit the table, which is too small for the complete poster.

This animal poster is charming, but a bit more childish than what I want. However, the jungle theme is similar in feeling and color.

got to cut! As I take the first slice I say to myself, "Look, it's only paper. If it doesn't work, it doesn't work." So I guess what I'm saying is that you must have courage. There's no looking back. Just forge ahead. And pray a little.

This poster is available through the Museum of Modern Art bookstore, 11 West 53 Street, New York, N.Y. 10019.

One good thing about this poster is that it has so much greenery that almost anywhere I cut into it, it would look natural. There isn't any pattern to match up or places that would look awkward if cut down the middle. I had only a vague plan when I started, and the design just emerged as I went along.

The gold trim was removed first because I found it distracting. Where the edges of the poster come down over the sides of the table, it is necessary to cut the leaves so that they look natural—sort of growing over onto the sides. Never throw away scraps. You can use everything from this poster. Wait and see.

There was a part in the front that I didn't care for and it didn't fall well on the table corner, so I lopped it right out leaving a big gaping hole. I also thought Mr. Rousseau's name should be in there, but when I was through I had second thoughts about that—I don't think he would have been too happy about someone tampering with his design. From the right-hand side of the poster I cut the large cluster of leaves containing the signature and dropped it into the hole. Now you can't even tell that anything was missing.

Using all the leftover pieces I began to embellish. All the possible leaves and flowers that could be saved were cut out. Leaves and stems are always good to save. They come in so handy for fillers when you need a bit of grass here and there. With this poster there was plenty left over, and I tried to use every bit of it. Whenever possible it is best to use all your cutouts from one source. In this way you will have an overall evenness in color, texture, thickness, and value. If you want to leave it as a simple project, you could just do the top piece and trim it all around with a razor blade. But why stop there when you can move on to bigger and better things. The legs just happened. I kept gluing pieces on as it seemed to look right. There was no specific plan other than to keep them airy with bits and pieces of

When the design is larger than the object it must be cut and designed to fit.

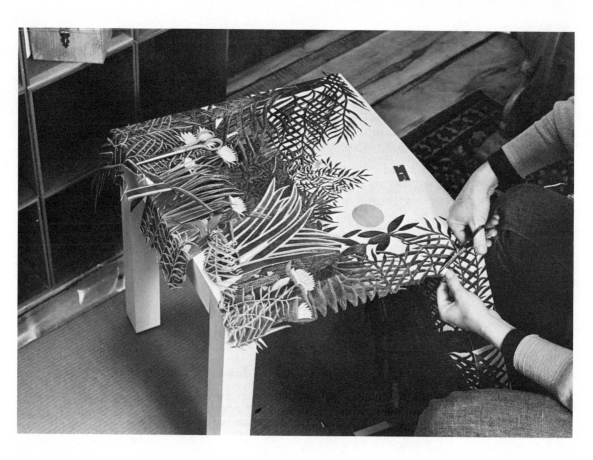

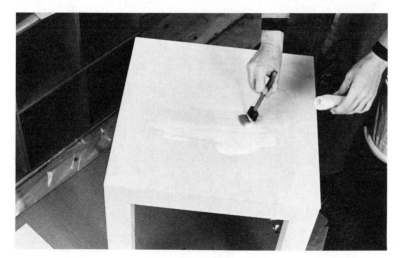

Brush glue across top of Parson's table.

Pull the design tightly with one hand while smoothing it down with the other.

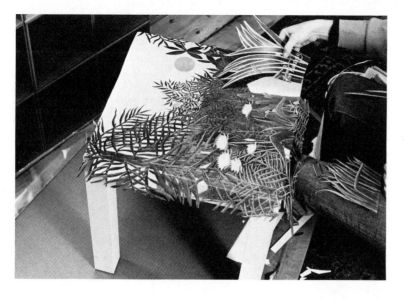

Fill blank space with cut out leaves.

Smooth down design by
rolling over it with brayer.

Cut out excess pieces to
use on the legs.

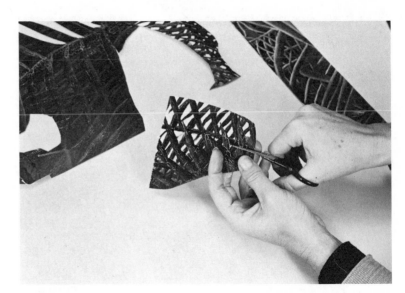

Sliver grasses so that they
can be placed here and
there where needed.

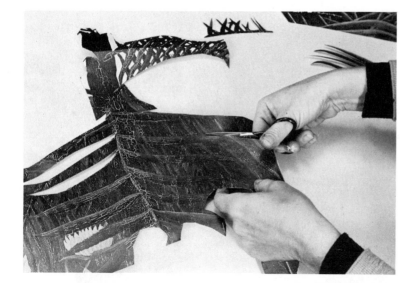

Large green areas provide long stems for the legs.

Sliver fat blades so that they are more delicate.

greenery. This isn't always so smart unless you have had some experience. It is safer and will make you feel more secure if you have a plan.

The animals were strictly an afterthought, and I wish they had been a forethought. I'll explain in a minute. Back to the leaves and things for the legs. First I took all those large and rather ugly leaves and one by one cut them into slivers. This is a trick (one that doesn't require any magic) my mother invented, and I think it's one of the best to have up your sleeve.

Using your scissors, cut very thin slivers from the top to just before the base of the leaf. Shape each piece if you

Large leaves can be slivered to use for blades of grass.

want. They don't all have to be straight. Curve a couple. Make them pointed and narrow at the top, widening at the base. Just the way blades of grass appear. You can do this with stems, leaves, branches, even a piece of green paper. I love it, don't you? This is how the designs were created for the legs. Some leaves were cut fatter to look more jungly; others to be grassy. These blades are also great for hiding imperfections, such as missing stems on large pink flowers. Okay, now back to the animals.

Where did they come from? When I started this project there was that darling French poster filled with crazy adorable animals. Remember? Since the animals were too large and would also give the table a childish look that I wasn't after, I didn't use it.

When I finished with the grasses and finishing touches on the legs I stood back and looked. Something was missing. My signature that says it's mine, or that certain "look" when I know the project is right, wasn't there. Until that point I would not be completely satisfied. Remember I told you that as you develop a style you'll find this in your own work. While each project may be totally different, there will be a similarity that makes all the pieces yours. Well, that something was not yet achieved. The animals! Why not use small animals that were the right scale for this scene? I felt that to keep the jungle effect, the leaves and flowers, etc., should be the dominant scene and the animals should be slightly camouflaged. A couple of years ago I had designed a series of animals and had them printed. They were perfect. I discarded rabbits, chinchillas, deer, raccoons, and many other darling small animals because they aren't found in a jungle. But the giraffe, zebra, hippo, and tigers and lions seemed closer to fitting in the environment.

This is why I'm sorry I didn't plan to use them before

The grasses are placed in front and back of the giraffe so that he is not plunked down awkwardly.

The animals are cut apart so that they appear to be coming out of the jungle. More leftover pieces of the poster are used on the other legs.

I had already glued the overall design in place. It would have been nice to have the animals in and out of the bush with grasses growing in front and back of them. By no longer having this option I had to cut the animals apart and place them in ways to make them look natural. Just plunking them down on top of everything would have been flat and dull. Also peculiar looking. So I had to cut off heads and parts of bodies and arrange them that way. My favorite is the gorilla hanging from a branch. His hand had to be cut in such a way as to make it appear as though he's holding onto a branch. The butterfly coming at the hippo was added on since he looked silly with a gaping mouth. Right over Henri Rousseau's name came my tiger. I wanted to do more. A snake twining up a sprig, a few bugs here and there, but I didn't have them and I was anxious to continue. I tried to find a pink bow for the elephant's tail and a little mouse on his trunk would have been a nice touch. A monkey riding on the giraffe's back would have really pleased me.

More animals were added on the legs. When you do a project like this take your time to find animals that will be just the right size, and for your own sake, or art's sake,

The tiger's head was cut off and placed so that the tiger seems to be walking through the grass.

plan it out first so that your finished piece will be exactly the way you want it to be.

I used polyurethane for this table instead of varnish because it produces an extremely hard finish, and the table might be abused with use. However, a varnish finish will protect the table just fine. I was a little careless when varnishing the legs and there are some drip marks. It is best when doing legs of a table or chair to set the piece on something so that dust and particles from the floor won't stick to the finish while it is drying. The finish can be floated across the top, but there should be light shining on the piece in such a way that you can see any places you have missed. This is sometimes easy to do when working on a large surface. Apply a much thinner coat of finish to the legs. Between six and ten coats is about right for this project. The sanding and steel wool rubbing between coats is done the same way as with all the other decoupage projects. Apply your wax at the end for protection. No antiquing is necessary here.

The butterfly was added so that the hippo wouldn't be left with a gaping mouth.

A director's chair or two

A director's chair is not an easy problem to tackle. As a matter of fact, in this case it took me two tries before I had it right. The shape doesn't lend itself to many designs, but I wanted it to have a fresh, springtime look. When I did the first one I didn't want to overload it with greens because the seat and back were so green. I was reading an article in a British magazine and came across an illustration that seemed as though it might fit well. Since the leaves were dark green, I didn't think that the type would show through. The biggest concern was whether there was enough for the whole project?

This can sometimes be a problem when you're doing a large piece. You need enough of the same kind of illustration or print for the entire project, or it will be extremely difficult to make the designs work together.

The pieces of the vines were cut apart so that I could stretch the leaves and have enough for both arms. This was as far as I could go with these leaves. Since they are fairly stylized—not realistic—I was concerned about using realistic leaves for the rest.

From a bird book that I cherish I cut some leaves and a bird that were close in color value. They were to be used on the bottom portion, away from the arms, so they seemed workable.

The overall effect that I wanted to achieve was a bit of a fantasy with unreal leaves and the big bird, so I added a few more fantasy touches. By placing a rabbit at the foot of the vines it became obvious that reality was not my goal. He is about one fourth the size of the bird. From one of the nursery books that I collect and cut from with extreme frugality, I cut a cricket in a tuxedo and top hat, a grasshopper napping under a strawberry bush, and an oversized dragonfly. On the front of each side is a tiny illustration of a path leading up to a castle. The castle in the distance is smaller than any of the critters. What I really should have had was a little character climbing up the vine with the castle in the sky. This chair tells a story. Any one you want to make up is fine.

The other director's chair is more sophisticated (although that's a word that probably should be defined). It has leaves twining around every rung. It was meant to look as though vines have taken over and made a permanent home here. If you want to do the exact same design, the vines and leaves were all cut from one book of trees and pieced together as I went along. While this chair goes with the other, it is different in feeling. This chair can be seen on the color pages.

A design should be pieced together only where there isn't enough to completely wrap around each leg or arm because you want the leaves to match where possible. If each piece is too different, it will not look as though they are twining. At times pieces had to be cut apart and stems added to make it look continuous. The feeling of twining was to be ever present. On this chair it is difficult to see the little bugs and butterflies since they were kept subtle. I deliberately used green caterpillars and natural-colored bugs so that they would be camouflaged. Sometimes it's fun to discover something after looking at it for a while. Subtle touches are what personalize a piece.

The first chair was varnished with a matte finish. This dulls and yellows the finish slightly. It turns the stark white of the paint into an ivory look. After several coats of varnish the chair was antiqued so lightly that it is barely preceptible.

The second chair was coated with a flat polymer medium. This is a water-base finish that dries in minutes. I used this because I was not working in my studio and had to leave the chair each day after I worked on it. There was no way to leave it totally undisturbed, and since the floor was carpeted the dust caused by people constantly walking would destroy a long-drying varnish finish. The polymer goes on murky white, but dries clear and doesn't yellow. It is a marvelous product for a quick cover, it isn't messy, and you can apply several coats in a day. It must be applied more carefully than varnish because it doesn't even out. In other words, the finish isn't as smooth. I use a poly-foam brush to apply this so that I can avoid brush strokes. After coating the entire chair go over it with your brush very lightly just to even it out. The water-base varnish or polymer medium comes in a matte finish or glossy and can be purchased in an art supply or craft store.

After applying two or three coats sand lightly just as with varnish. The problem with this finish is that it is not as professional looking as a varnish finish, nor does it hold up as well. You cannot, however, use this water-base finish and then apply varnish over it. The varnish is an oil base

A climbing vine makes a good design for the arm of a director's chair.

Antiquing adds a touch of accent and creates depth to the design if applied carefully.

Wipe away most of the antiquing leaving traces around the design. This will change the flat white color to a soft ivory.

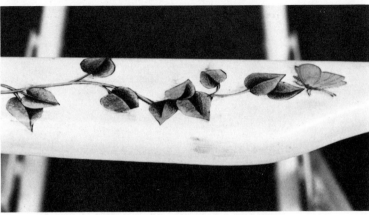

The difference is quite subtle, but the antiquing definitely adds to the piece.

and will pull right off of the water finish. When using the polymer medium clean your brush in water after each use.

When buying materials learn to read labels carefully. All decoupage materials can't automatically be assumed to work together. Not all products are compatible. You must read labels to find out a little about the materials you plan to use. This is the only way to insure a perfect decoupage project every time. If you aren't sure, do a test on a piece of wood. Part of learning how to do a craft is becoming familiar with the materials used.

Decoupage on metal

Decoupage is as lovely on metal as it is on wood. A metal tray makes a good project because it is a flat surface and there are many design possibilities. Trays provide a good opportunity to use borders. Greeting cards have lovely borders that can be cut out and pieced around the edge of the tray. You might want to use a print of a piece of fruit. Or wild flowers growing from the bottom and branching up the sides would be lovely. If the tray is rusted or the paint that is on it isn't in good condition, sand it so that the surface is ready for repainting. If you use a paint made especially for metal, such as Rust-Oleum, you will have an excellent base for your decoupage. A water-base paint, such as latex or acrylic paint, may also be used. This dries much faster but is not as good.

After you have selected your design and applied it, coat the entire tray with varnish just as when working on wood. Do not use shellac or lacquer for a tray as they will not hold up under spills of water or alcohol. Use wood varnish for your tray. When varnishing, you not only cover the top surface but the bottom as well. If the entire tray is not sealed with varnish, moisture is apt to seep in from the bottom when the tray is cleaned and cause your design to lift.

If you have a decoupaged piece that has been ruined in this way, it may have been for several reasons. If a design has begun to pull away from the surface of the box or plaque, etc., even though you made it more than three months ago, it may be due to the fact that when the design was originally applied the paint was not dry enough. Or there may have been too much glue left under the design. One coat of varnish may not have been thoroughly dry before the next coat was applied. If any one of these things happened as the print dried under the varnish, the design would begin to shrink and pull away from the surface it had been applied to. This can happen months after the project has been completed. To avoid this, let each step dry thoroughly before going on to the next.

If you are faced with a rusty metal object that you would like to decoupage, the first thing to do is to sand off as much rust as possible. Then paint the object with a rust-preventing paint. Rust-Oleum is good for this and comes in a variety of colors. Use an enamel rather than water-base paint. Once dry your designs can then be applied and varnished over all. Enamel paint takes twenty-four hours to dry. If you use a water-base paint, handle your object carefully so that the paint will not chip before you have had a chance to protect it with varnish.

Tin snuff cans can be decoupaged simply.

Snuff cans are a little bit bigger than film cans. They are also a more handy size and better looking. They are made of tin and are often hard to find, but they make really cute decoupage projects. This idea was given to me along with three snuff cans by Virginia Haith. Since they are made of shiny metal, they should first be sanded before attempting to paint or varnish them. They can be painted with a water-base paint, or you can decoupage right on the tin. These small cans provide excellent easy-to-make gifts or first projects. Use them on a sewing table to hold buttons in one, pins in another, and needles in a third. Make one to hold earrings and rings, or use them for paper clips or push pins on a desk.

I put graphic numbers 1, 2, 3 on mine using Letraset type, available at art supply stores. You could also use letters. If you can't do it any other way, cut letters or numbers from a magazine.

Film cans can be painted bright colors and decoupaged with magazine cutouts.

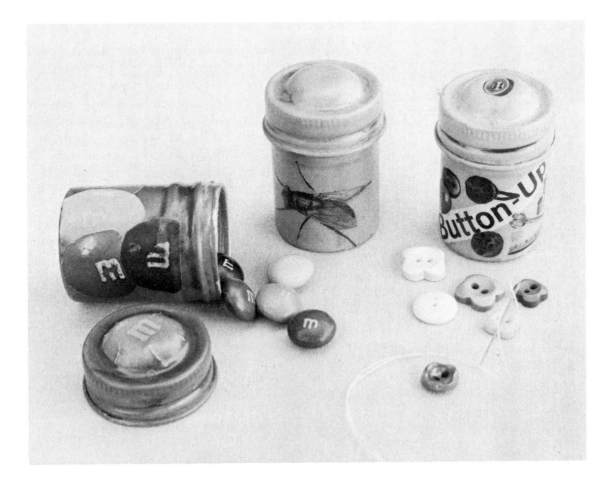

First sand the can, then apply the letter or number you choose. The design you select should be rather small to fit the scale of these items. Apply the letter or number before choosing the design so that you can arrange around it. I used very delicate pink flowers with thin grassy leaves. I cut many of the leaves apart so that some could be placed on either side of the numbers. If you haven't painted, you might like to use a glossy varnish to retain the shiny look of the original can. If you choose to paint the cans, do not apply paint where the top and bottom come together. You will need two or three coats of paint.

The varnish does not adhere on metal the same way as it did on the wood. It takes many more coats and must be applied with thin rather than thick applications. It will take twenty-four hours for each coat to dry, and you can count on at least six coats of varnish.

How to decoupage a trunk for under $5.00

Now that you're hooked on designing with posters there's a project that can be done in no time and for practically nothing, and combines posters with decoupaging on metal.

If you have an empty camp trunk around, or if you are presently using it for storage, drag it out. If you are going off to college this is a great project to do for your dorm. And finally, if you like the idea and don't have a trunk, you can get one for about fifteen dollars at most Army and Navy supply stores. But then, of course, you have to ignore the title because you just went and blew the entire budget.

You can use the trunk as is or, if you like, change the color. If you decide to paint, use any paint that you have left over from something else. My trunk was pretty old so I painted it dark green with latex paint. If you are going to paint it, you must first sand all exposed surfaces. This will remove any wax or oily substance that might be a protective covering already on the trunk. Try not to paint over the hinges and locks. Take extra care going around them. On the other hand, if hinges are ugly, you can paint over them. Use an inexpensive polyfoam brush for this. If you use a dark color, only one coat is necessary. If you are painting it white and it was black, you will need at least two coats. Since most of the surface will be covered, don't paint unless it is in really crumby condition. The poster that you choose could be any one that you already have or you can buy one that costs about two dollars. Some are even less. Almost everyone has a poster that can be used, but if you are buying one, try to get one that is horizontal so that it will fit to the shape of the trunk. The one that I used is very common and I've seen it often in stationery and bookstores. The paper is very thick so I used regular scissors to trim it down a little. I cut out the border and around outer flowers to make it look less like a poster and more as though it had been designed for the trunk. If there are tiny areas to get into, use a cuticle scissors for this. Then lay the poster design on the trunk to see which way it will fit best. I cut the bottom portion of this poster away and pieced it onto the front rather than leaving it overlapping from top to bottom. Because the paper was thick it was easier to glue it this way. If you are using a thinner paper, the design can be glued right onto the trunk and later cut with a razor blade

A metal doll's trunk designed and decoupaged by Ruth Linsley.

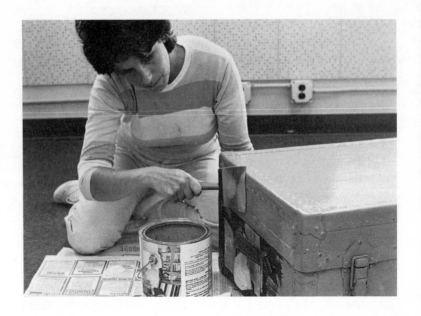

where the trunk opens. Of course this means cutting out areas where all the hinges and locks are and you have to play around with it so that the design won't look awkward. When choosing your poster keep this in mind.

You can use white glue or, if the paper is super thick, 3M Super Strength adhesive has more holding power. Be sure that all edges are securely down and do a lot of patting, pressing, and rolling out of air bubbles and spots where glue has collected. This will take some time but it's important. When the design is secured you might want to add an extra touch. I used 3M decorator tape in a gold color to trim the top of the trunk. This gave it a gold metallic look. This is totally optional and only if you like the look and want to spend the extra thirty-nine cents. Now you are ready to varnish. A high-gloss varnish is just right for this project. Apply three or four coats of varnish allowing each to dry overnight. Sand the last coat lightly with fine sandpaper as before and apply a coat of wax for protection. This will give you a very shiny contemporary-looking project. If you want to go farther, you can line the inside with wallpaper, wrapping paper, or Contact adhesive paper. The only real expense for this project is the poster and varnish which you may already have.

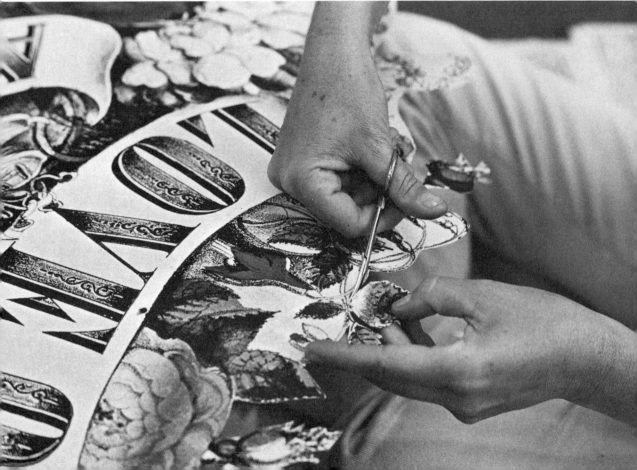

A doll's
trunk

I know that many people are collectors. They save everything. This isn't the same way that I mean saving when I talk about saving cutouts. That's a whole different thing. So all of you who are collectors will know what I mean when I tell you that my mother is a collector. The doll's trunk that she decoupaged is real proof. I haven't played with dolls for a lot longer than I'm going to admit to, so I really was surprised when she showed me her latest project. We don't see each other too often. Only when I'm working on a book and call her to see what new decoupage projects she's up to. This doll's trunk is one I've never seen done. It was mine when I was a kid and I don't think they even make them anymore. At least not in metal.

The trunk had been quite rusty and was painted with an enamel after the rust was removed. The designs are on all sides as well as the top and look well from any angle. This piece can be used as a little end table or just for decoration. If it weren't designed on end, it could have been used the other way. There are lots of ways that this project could have been designed.

Boxes

Where to find them

I almost tricked myself this time. Ever since I began to do decoupage I have worked primarily on boxes. Any kind of box or wood container that has entered my door has been turned into a decoupage project. I dream about boxes, and find that I almost design them in my sleep.

It would have been easy to give you a book filled with boxes, but since I have already done that, I set out in this book to explore other areas of decoupage. I got so carried away that I almost forgot how lovely boxes are and how popular they have been. Most of you will probably be making boxes; certainly not decoupaging boats. Craft shops are loaded with a great variety of boxes, and if you are already doing decoupage, I'm sure you have been looking and collecting some on your own. Aside from local craft shops, many manufacturers have mail order catalogues, and you will find boxes often advertised in national magazines. Once again, garage sales are a good place to pick up wood items to decoupage.

Unusual wood items are harder to find than the ones that are mass produced. If you like to poke around antique stores, this is a fun way to find something, but it's getting terribly expensive.

Jon and I headed up toward Vermont one morning. It started out to be one of those glorious fall weekends. The sun was shining, but the cold crisp air of late October warned of winter coming. The leaves were just turning and the countryside was dotted with grazing cows and barns in much worse condition than ours. If you're from anywhere

*Antique shops have great
things to decoupage.*

else in the country, I don't think I can describe that feeling of driving along a New England road in the fall. The grandeur of nature is overwhelming. The colors alone should be enough to make you want to rush home to create your next decoupage project of rust and brown and russet and orange and yellow and wine and pink. We were looking for some out-of-the-way places to rediscover. We've traveled this area so much that it is getting harder and harder to be original. When we are getting stale it's a great way to clean house and start anew. Just driving through upper New England slowly makes you think of new ideas.

Antique shops are plentiful, and no matter how many times we stop in Stockbridge and I say, "Never again, it's getting too crowded," we always seem to make it through

Local craft shops have a large variety of boxes but look for unusual objects in out-of-the-way places.

Old hinges, locks, and handles can be adapted for purses and boxes.

this delightful little town in Massachusetts. Where the endless supplies come from is a question for George Grotz, but there is always something for everyone no matter how often you stop.

We never spend lots of money. That's one of the "rules." If you get something great but spend a fortune, it sort of takes the fun out of it. Especially for decoupage. Therefore, we don't feel we have to know a great deal about the worth of things. We go on native intelligence. After all, if you spend three dollars for something that's made of wood (never mind what it is), what difference does it make if you're over- or underpaying? You bought it because you saw something in it that you felt was worth paying the three bucks for. We usually decide ahead of time just how much we'll spend, and five dollars for an item means we considered it something pretty hot. With decoupage you want to make something better. If you pay a fortune for it, it's probably better to begin with.

The biggest problem we have is that too often I buy something to decoupage, and when I get it home find that it's too beautiful as is. This was the case with an old handmade tool—a beautiful T square—that we bought that weekend. The handle is made of wood and has a brass decoration holding it together and brass edging. The handle was too lovely to decoupage, so I didn't. For a dollar I also found a slightly rusty metal pail which will be great to decoupage. It has a handle and will be good for holding letters, or as a planter. I like useful items.

Lovely old brass drawer pulls make exquisite purse handles. Much nicer than the plastic ones available in craft stores. Sometimes you can find interesting catches and locks for boxes. There was a little piece of wood lying on a table. It was an unusual shape and very smooth. A great key chain.

Finding items to decoupage this way gives additional meaning to your project. If you are on a trip or a short jaunt, take a slight detour. If you find something to make after you get home, it will be a nice remembrance of your trip. It's also fun to make your hobby part of your everyday life.

File or recipe boxes of wood or metal are often tucked away, and now is the time to pull them out and restore them. An old rusted metal file box can be made over with decoupage and will look better than it did originally.

An old pail will make a lovely plant holder or catchall once it is decoupaged.

How to make gramp's boxes

I have received many letters from people all over the country asking about the boxes that I use for decoupage. When I was lecturing in Florida a very sweet woman came up and introduced herself. She said that she had enjoyed my work and had looked forward to meeting me, but what she really wanted was to meet my grandfather and learn all his secrets for box making.

My grandfather, who is in his ninetieth year, has been making all my boxes by hand since I decoupaged my first box. He is an incredible man and can do much more than make boxes. He is an accomplished painter of paintings

and houses, and he can prune a hedge like no one else. He can tell stories about the "good old days" and remember things that not too many others can. But since I don't get to see him much now, our conversations are confined to correspondence, and he writes some of the sharpest, funniest letters I've ever read. As a matter of fact, he helped us rebuild our barn through the mail all winter long. While he's up on everything he claims that his greatest difficulty is keeping up with my grandmother who is the prettiest and most sociable lady in Hollywood, according to him. I'd have to say that my grandparents are two of the most remarkable people I know, and anyone who has seen my grandfather's boxes would have to agree he knows what he's doing. They aren't always perfect, but that's what makes them so charming.

If you are interested in making your own boxes or just trying one for the fun of it, this is how to do it. No power tools are necessary since Gramp and I are of the same Yankee schooling. Do it as inexpensively as possible. Why he's even been known to make a box out of old wooden slats from venetian blinds.

When I first asked Gramp to write this chapter he said that he would jot down notes when making the boxes. Usually, the way we work is that I drop him a note with a sketch for a new size box or boxes and tell him how many I want of each. We don't believe in any complicated system. Mostly, however, they are our standard ones and I simply say, "Hey, Gramp, I need 4 half rounds and 2 pencil boxes, no changes," and two weeks later my package arrives. Sometimes I get an idea for something like a thread holder or plant holder, in which case I scribble a note with an approximate size and ask for suggestions. I usually get his ideas back in the form of two different sizes all made up. Pretty neat wouldn't you say?

Well, after I asked Gramp to make notes I got a scrawled letter back. Gramp usually says what he has to say, no more or less. This note simply read, "Dear Leslie, I enjoy making the boxes better than writing about them." I then suggested sending him a tape recorder, and he could talk as he had ideas and then send me the tapes. This wasn't too appealing to Gramp.

So from his sketchy notes I have constructed some directions. If there are parts missing it is because Gramp decided to keep a few secrets for his old age, but you'll get the gist.

Making a box with
a half-round or
elliptical lid

This core or skeleton is made of ¼″ plywood or any wood of the same thickness. The parts are put together with white glue and ½″ brads. The wood used to cover the front and bend over the top and down the back is called doorskin, usually used on flush doors. It is three ply about ⅛″ thick. Cut a piece a little longer than the box to be covered, with the grain running down its length. To allow bending, remove one ply by sanding. Cover the core surface with glue and use brads where needed. Starting with front of box, cover the sides and top with the doorskin.

As the work proceeds sand all edges smooth. After gluing use clamps or weights to assist bonding. Then mark a line where you want to separate the lid from the lower part. Cut with a hand saw. Then sand edges smooth and apply the surface hinges and a catch or lock at the front.

The outer covering, or doorskin, is usually made of Philippine mahogany with a high-gloss finish and does not require further work.

A slip-on cover

A slip-on cover for a box is made by lining the lower part of the box with thin wood. This is when Gramp uses those old venetian blind slats. The lining should extend ¼″ to ⅜″ above the edge. Boxes with mitered corners can easily be made with the use of a power saw set at a 45° angle. When the inside of the box is divided in sections, use thin wood. Where the compartment walls cross each other cut wood, as in Figure 1. Cut notches on the insides of the box to hold the ends of the compartment wall in place. Glue the edges of the compartment walls.

Basically, all boxes are built the same way. They differ only where the tops are shaped differently. It's best to make a rough sketch or plan before starting. Where a fine finish is desired, veneers of all fine woods can be bought at Constantine & Co., 2050 Eastchester Road, New York, N.Y. 10461.

To make the half-round or trunk-shaped box, Gramp makes the core of ¼″ plywood. The parts are put together with white glue and ½″ brads.

No fancy tools are used. The wood that is used for the top is bent from front to back. This piece is called the doorskin. It is usually used on flush doors.

This piece is three ply about ⅛″ thick. To allow bending, remove one ply by sanding. This piece should be a little longer than the core that you are covering.

Glue the doorskin down with lots of glue and hold with a vise. Use ½″ brads to secure the piece.

When the top is bonded mark a line
where you will separate the lid from the
bottom portion. This box is made as one
piece and then cut apart. Use a handsaw
for this.

Sand all rough edges when finished.
Gramp does this on his rigged up sanding
wheel; however, it can be done by hand.

Sometimes Gramp doesn't cut these
perfectly straight and they have a unique
charm because of the handmade quality.

Fancy hinges and a catch are then added
to the outside. If you do not want the back
hinges to show, you might use a hidden
piano hinge or countersink your hinges
inside the back of the bottom half.

Designing
a box

Where do you get ideas for designs to put on the boxes? We already have talked about the various places to buy prints, cards, paper, etc. But there are influences all around us that can become an inspiration for a decoupage project. Nature, of course, is the most obvious. Often I will see a field of wild flowers, and if I squint, I can narrow the scene down so that I can visualize a portion of it all designed on a box. You have to learn to block out much of what you see so that you can pick out a simple idea.

In Nantucket, where the natural setting is so overwhelming, it is easy to set out on a bike trip and find inspirational settings. But you don't need to be in a romantic or exotic or unusual area for this to happen. It's just a matter of narrowing down. Look out of your window and start daydreaming. Even looking at a huge black-topped driveway can sometimes prove interesting. Once I saw a tiny blue chicory growing right up out of a black-topped parking lot. Okay, that isn't exactly awe-inspiring, but you get what I'm saying. The way things grow naturally is a good guide for designing things on a box.

The Old Mill in Nantucket is a famous landmark on the island, and one day looking through an old nursery book I saw an illustration of a windmill. I must have gone through this book over a hundred times, but I had only seen what I wanted to see, and wasn't interested in windmills before. Now I decided to make a windmill box and photograph it right by the Old Mill. The background color of the box would be yellow because the mill was colored with yellows, oranges, and a touch of blue. I decided to use a box that was small and would be almost completely covered by the mill because I didn't have anything that I felt could go with it. There was one problem, however. The picture had an old man asleep at the foot of the mill, and when he was cut away it left a funny gap in front of the mill. This type of problem should never eliminate the use of an illustration that you like. Just learn to doctor it up. I thought a cluster of blue chicory wild flowers could fill in the space nicely. These were not too hard to find in one of my wild flower books, in just the right size. However, the paper was very thick, and if placed so that the flowers overlapped onto the mill, it would be too thick and require endless coats of varnish. Even then it would be an uneven

surface. Often you may find a print or a cute greeting card that you'd like to use, but the paper is too thick. If it is thick, it will be difficult to cut evenly and will have a choppy outline rather than a smooth professional look.

To thin paper is quite simple. All it means is that a layer of paper is peeled off the back of the card. To do this, carefully pull away a corner of the back using your cuticle scissors or a razor blade. Then slowly, so that you won't rip the front, peel off a layer, thus making the card thin enough to work with. One layer is all you can re- move without danger of ripping. If you find this difficult, take a clear piece of adhesive paper such as Contact paper which is available in any hardware or paint store. Place a piece on the back of the card to be thinned. Smooth it down with your hand so that it is stuck well. Lift a corner

This design is not complete in the front and needs additional cutouts to cover the uneven line.

Thinning or peeling a layer of paper.

so that the card and adhesive paper separate and continue to pull the adhesive paper off. A layer of the card will stick to the adhesive paper and the card will be thinned in a breeze. This can also be done with wedding and birth announcements.

When designing a box the prints should be chosen in relation to the size box on which they will be used. Remember that a box is a three-dimensional object unlike a plaque. You are working with a top and four sides, all of which should be interrelated. It is much more interesting if your designs come from the front and extend up onto the top and again over onto the sides. Or they could start on the top with bits and pieces extending over to include all sides, rather than working on each side as though it existed alone. With a plaque you are only interested in the flat surface—much like creating a painting. A box is different. If you are designing a bouquet of flowers on a box, you might start the stems from the front and extend them up onto the top. If the stems aren't long enough, add a

The oblong box is designed very simply; however, the leaves extend slightly over the edges to include the back and sides.

piece to extend them. A few petals or leaves could then trail down onto the sides. Most of all, it should look natural. If you are working on a small box, don't overpower it with a huge design. Remember that the object you are decoupaging is part of the design, not just the design itself. Small cutout designs would look awkward on a piece of furniture, for instance. Your design can be quite simple, or you might add more cutouts to make it more decorative.

Sometimes it's interesting to see how a print can work on two completely different objects. One of the prints that I use frequently is of a dandelion and two black-eyed Susans. On a small round trinket box it is necessary to use only part of the print, but on my pencil box the whole print works well, and I can even add a few leaves to make it fuller. A box can be designed in many different ways. Shirley Appy designed this box with the elegant simplicity of oriental design. She then added a brass catch and corners for interest. Color is another consideration. Often a design will suggest a mood, and the color can change this. For instance, daisies

When more wild flowers are added the design becomes busier. Part of the same design can also be used on a small round shape effectively.

always look fresh and young. When used against a yellow background the white petals show up and a bright yellow and white object is very gay looking. When used against a powder blue the whole piece changes to a cooler mood suggesting a sky background with the daisies growing wild. If the white petaled daisies were placed against a white background, the design would be far more subtle and sophisticated. White on white with green leaves can be very subtle and elegant.

I used red poppies on a lap desk that was painted a pale blue. It is a nice combination, but if I had put the red flowers on a white background it would have looked entirely different.

The designs should follow the lines of the box. If you are working on an oblong box, the designs should go across the box in a natural way. A flower such as an iris really

An entirely different look is achieved with this elegant oriental design created by Shirley Appy.

shouldn't start with the bottom of the stem at one end and grow across the top to the other. The design should go in the same direction that one views the box when using it. You shouldn't have to turn the box sideways to see the design right side up. The shape of a box or container will often inspire a design. The chicory growing up and around this catchall seems just right for the shape.

When working on something that is a little bit different, such as the three-tiered letter holder, it presents a unique design problem. While it is one boxlike object, there are three separate parts, and although they are designed separately they must go together. Gramp made the wall-hanging letter holder for my mother to decoupage, and Jon photographed it on the very day that they were moving to Florida, just in time so that we could include it in the book.

The chicory flowers design well on this round catchall.

166

To achieve a consistent look in the design, you should use the same source for all your cutouts for an object like this. While the design does not flow from one section to the next, it has the same theme and thus the overall feeling is of unity. The little field animals in the moss and ferns carry from top to bottom. This is a nice item and can only be fully appreciated when not in use. Unfortunately, the letters cover the design.

Wooden letter holder made by Gramp, designed by Ruth Linsley.

Lining a box
with paper

If you have chosen to line your box rather than paint the inside, save this step for last. Choose a print that will go well with your outer design. The lining could be done with wallpaper, wrapping paper, Contact paper, felt, or fabric. Velvet is lovely for a jewelry box, and Shirley's oriental box is lined with brocade. Be especially careful when selecting a lining paper to avoid paper that is very thin. If the paper is too thin, it will tear and wrinkle when applied.

A surprise lining can add interest to your box. When choosing a paper for lining, try to find something that is a contrasting color to the design. Pick up one of the least used accent colors on your box and use it inside. It is interesting to open a very subtly colored box and find an exciting color leap out at you from inside. Most boxes are not very big so try to avoid large prints. The small overall patterns are best. Take your box with you when choosing a lining so that you can see the effect together.

You'll need glue, a ruler, and scissors to do the job. When you have everything together measure all areas to be lined.

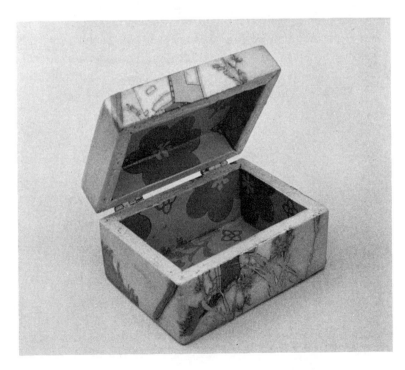

A contrasting orange and yellow lining is used on the Old Mill box.

Using a ruler and pen measure on the paper to be used each piece to the exact dimensions. Cut each one out and glue them in place in the box. I usually cut the sides slightly larger than the measure so that they will overlap a little. The excess can be trimmed later with a razor blade or cuticle scissors. Put the sides in first and then the large pieces for the inside top and bottom. They should be cut as exact as possible. The same paper can be cut to cover the outside bottom, or you might place a piece of felt on it. Simply draw around the outer edge of the box directly on the felt. Cut out this piece. Spread glue on the bottom of the box and lay the felt piece on it. Smooth it out with your hand and trim any excess with cuticle scissors. If you are working on a plaque, you would do the same thing for the back of the plaque to protect the wall.

When you have completed the lining apply a coat of varnish over the entire lining to protect it. Also, if you have antiqued the outside, it is usually a good idea to do the inside so that it will be consistent. Leave antiquing dirt in the corners and let it dry as before. Put a coat of varnish over the antiquing, let it dry, sand and rub with fine steel wool. Apply wax inside the same way you did to the outside.

If you line the box before you start varnishing the outside, you can varnish the inside and out at the same time. Prop it open slightly so that it dries inside and out. This saves time. Do not prop it open too much or the top will have drip marks. If you are lining with fabric, finish the entire outside, varnish, and antique before lining. If you don't, you are sure to get something gooky on that lining.

Lining a box with fabric

Fabric is tricky to work with and you must select it carefully. If the fabric is delicate and thin, such as silk, you need to be extra, extra careful. Measure each side as with the paper. Then cut each piece about ¼″ larger all around than the area to be lined. Next, cut pieces of cardboard, such as shirt board, the exact size—or a little bit smaller—for each side of your box. Apply glue to one side of each piece of cardboard, one at a time, and glue it to the center of the wrong side of each piece of fabric. Fold the edges of fabric over the cardboard and glue them to the cardboard to keep the edges from raveling. Keep your fingers free from glue while doing this, especially with velvet. Apply glue to the back side of each piece and press it in place in the box. Each piece should fit exactly. Try each one in place before gluing because as each piece is added to the box the space becomes smaller and the next piece with the extra little bit that the fabric adds may be too snug. In this case, your cardboard pieces should be trimmed. If you use felt, there is no need to use the cardboard pieces since the felt doesn't unravel.

Shirley Appy lined her oriental box with green brocade.

Unusual projects

Decoupage
a lamp shade

It is very easy to decoupage a lamp shade as long as it is fairly smooth. There is no painting involved, and you may choose to forget about varnishing. My mother made this shade for an antique lamp she had in the living room. You cut out your paper designs just as with any other decoupage project, but it is a good idea to keep your designs light and airy. If you have the shade too covered with cutouts, it reduces the amount of light that comes through. Plan your design carefully so that you have exactly enough to cover all the way around. When you do your gluing, hold your hand inside the shade and with the other hand press against the design so that it will be secure. Now you can apply a coat or two of varnish to protect the prints. I don't recommend lots of varnish on this project because it cuts down on the light and it isn't really necessary.

A three-paneled
screen

Last year I decoupaged a screen for *House Beautiful.* (See color page 1.) They would have been very happy if it were room size, but I wasn't quite that ambitious. What I made was a small nine-inch-high screen for a desk. It is used as a decoration and to keep letters and junk out of sight. This is the way to make it.

Lamp shade design by Ruth Linsley.

Each panel is nine inches high and four and a half inches wide. They are made from ¼" wood. You can make them yourself, have them cut at a lumberyard or find ready-made ones in some craft shops. The panels for mine were painted white, but yours should be any color to fit with your room. Using acrylic paint, each panel should be painted and sanded smooth. The rims and back should be painted as well to keep them from warping. Choose a print that creates a scene so that you can design it to go across the three panels. Or you might place three separate but relating subjects on the individual sections. Once you have chosen and cut out your pieces lay the panels down side by side, flat. Now glue the designs in place. If the pieces overlap from one panel to the next, cut it at the separation with a razor blade. Be sure that the panels line up perfectly when gluing your designs in place. If they don't, when you put the panels together, the design will be out of alignment.

Continue to finish each section in the same way that you would do a plaque. Lightly apply antiquing in the corners and around your designs leaving the major portion of the screen clean. When you have finished you are ready to hinge the panels together. With such thin panels of wood it is difficult to apply narrow enough hinges without splitting the wood. Cloth hinges, which can be found in hardware or frame shops, work quite well. These hinges are actually a strip of gauzelike material that is glued on either side of the two panels that come together. With this hinge the screens can only open in one direction; other kinds of hinges are made to swing in either direction. If this movement is desirable, you will have to find a hinge that is narrow enough to do the job.

If you do not want such delicate panels, the screen will be easier to make. Thicker wood is much more readily available in already finished and beveled edges. These can easily be hinged, and the exact hinges needed are no trouble to find in craft and hardware stores. It is the thin delicate screens in any size that are a bit of a nuisance to work with but add charming touches to a room.

Decoupage
on ceramic

The Bennington Potters make a heavy ceramic egg cup that costs approximately $2.50 and is perfect for decoupage. Even after it is decoupaged and coated with many layers of varnish it can still be used for soft-boiled eggs. It can't be put in the dishwasher, or at least I don't, but it can safely be washed by hand. And it looks so pretty on a shelf or table. I was really surprised at how well it works for decoupage. The shape is different and it is an easy and elegant gift to make. In this case, there is no painting involved as it is already white ceramic. I used regular Elmer's Glue-All just as I use on wood. The designs I chose were all wild flowers and berries. A butterfly was added to supply an accent color and interest. The designs all grow up from the bottom and extend almost to the top and around the cup. One of the cups has bright yellow buttercups on it with green leaves, one has very subtle almost brown berries, and the other has purple buds. Each has an entirely different look. If you aren't planning to use this for an egg cup, the inside can be lined with paper or fabric. It isn't easy to do this with the egg shape, but it can be done. A few wrinkles, but what are a few wrinkles among friends?

Ceramic eggs do not have to be painted before applying decoupage.

Decoupage under glass

Decoupage under glass is almost the same as decoupage on wood only in reverse. Rather than applying the design on top of the object you are placing it under. First, clean the surface of the glass. It might be an ash tray, a plate, coasters, a hurricane lamp, or the front of a clock. The project shown here was beautifully decoupaged by Jean Buck. Once you have cut out your designs and decided where to place them, apply a small drop of diluted white glue on the front of the design. Dilute the glue with a drop of water so that it will not be so thick. Press the design face up under the glass. Continue to press the design firmly in place forcing all the glue to spread and ooze out the sides. You can watch this happening because you can see it through the glass. When you apply a design to wood you just assume that everything is in place and that there is not too much or too little glue under your design. Don't worry if the glue is white between your cutout and the glass. As you press and work the glue out it will even out and dry clear. It takes longer to do decoupage under glass because you will take more time with the gluing.

When all your designs have been applied this way you are ready to paint. Using a small piece of sponge, dip it into the paint. Turn your glass face down, and using the water-base paint that was used on wood, dab it over the back of your print. It is very important that the designs are securely glued down on all edges. If there is any area that has been neglected, the paint will seep in under the print and ruin the face of it.

Once the first coat dries it will be spotty. Apply a second and, if need be, a third. If you are working on a coaster, you can cut out a piece of felt and apply it to the bottom right over the painted surface, thus completely avoiding varnishing. Or you can go ahead now and for protection varnish over the paint as you have done with everything else. Of course, you can't antique. So to summarize, first glue the print, face down, apply paint to back of the print, let dry, and apply varnish.

Photographs

Often people will ask me if photographs can be used. Of course they can, and there are many ways to use a favorite photo for a decoupage project. The first time I used a photograph was for a plaque to hang in my hallway. I mounted the color photograph on a plaque that was larger than the picture. There was a border of about one inch all the way around. I had first painted the plaque white before mounting the photo. The photograph I used was of an eighteen-month-old child so that the decoupage prints around it had to have a young feeling. I designed a border with delicate pink buds that were pasted around the edges and over onto the picture. Then approximately six coats of varnish were applied, but not antiquing. This is the simplest way to decoupage a photograph, but I don't find it particularly satisfying in terms of design.

The next time I worked with photographs I used one of a boy and one of a girl for a gift project. The idea was to do something with a photograph without spending any money. Well, hardly any money. If you happen to have a Sucrets tin, or similar size tin, around it won't cost anything at all. I used two Sucrets cough drop tins for this project. Water-base paint can be used but chips off easily when used on metal. Handle the object carefully once it has been painted. You have to do a careful paint job, and you must sand the box before you start. Once the varnish is applied the paint is protected. If you do a large metal project, you will first sand the metal inside and out. Then apply a coat of Rust-Oleum paint. You must let the coat of paint dry overnight, and you may need two coats. Clean your brush in mineral spirits. If you don't want to go to the trouble and expense (the paint costs more than a water-soluble paint), use a good acrylic paint and handle the object carefully, especially in the back where the top and bottom are hinged together. This is where the paint begins to peel off first because of the opening and closing. After a couple of coats of paint have been applied, you are ready to mount your picture. If you have to cut it up a bit to make it fit, do so. It's best to have it fit right on the top rather than to go over the sides. The paper is so thick and stiff that it doesn't adhere well when bent. Mine kept popping up in front where part of the picture lapped over. I also found that a strong glue such as 3M Super Strength glue is better to use on metal than a glue such as Elmer's or Sobo.

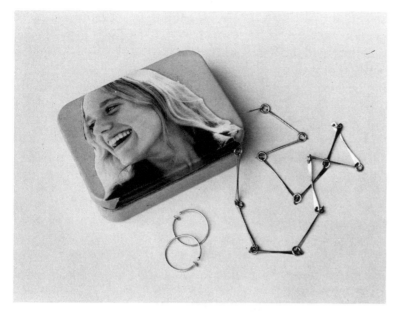

A Sucrets tin decoupaged with a black-and-white photo and lined with wallpaper.

If you wet a black-and-white photo until it is soaked, spread your glue on the tin, and then place your wet photo right on top, it will adhere best. Do not wet a color photo, only black and white. I made this mistake and had to re-touch the photograph where the color began to disappear. After the photograph is laid in place, take a clean cloth or slightly damp sponge and pat it down. As the photograph dries it will tighten up on the top of the box. A photograph is quite thick and needs several coats of varnish to cover it. When applying varnish only do the outside of the tin box if you are planning to line the inside. Be sure all sides are coated, then place the open box over a glass or jar so that it can dry on all sides at once. I applied five or six coats of varnish to mine. I did not antique these as I don't like to see antiquing on photographs. When I had completed the out-side I sanded lightly. If you sand too heavily, you will sand your picture off. After sanding apply a coat of paste wax the same way you do to a wooden object. The two boxes that I did are lined with wallpaper. You might like to do this or line them with wrapping paper or self-adhesive paper such as Contact. Even felt can be used. Be sure to pick a print that is small and an overall pattern. This is a tiny area that you will line so you can't use a large print. Either measure the inside of the box on the bottom and then all sides, or set the box on top of the paper and draw lines around the outside of each side and bottom and top. Then cut out all pieces to be used for the lining. Paste each piece in place and set it aside to dry. It is really fun to open a tiny box and find an exciting lining inside. Try to find a paper that either matches or contrasts to your outside color. If you've used a black-and-white photo, you can pick any color you want for the background. I used a burnt orange. For the color photo, I used pale blue. One lining is a yellow and orange print, the other is a yellow and blue small over-all print. These were just small bits of wallpaper samples. Apply a coat of varnish over the paper inside to protect it.

Photo collage
(a family portrait)

When we were in Nantucket last summer Jon and I were walking along some back roads one night. I remarked that I wished that I could use a photograph of one of the old houses in Nantucket for a project. We talked about this and the next day set out to take some pictures. While we were doing this the idea came to me to do something original with photographs. Since many people collect family photos I thought it would be fun to do a new kind of family portrait. It wasn't all that easy to find a really neat old house that was completely in the clear. Most of the houses had trees or a telephone pole right smack in the front yard. Naturally, my favorites. After several attempts we found this nice old house and decided it would be perfect for what I had in mind. Even the roof was in the clear and had all kinds of possibilities. My idea was to take photos that we had of family and friends and reduce or enlarge them to the size necessary to fit the people in the house. I cut out windows and placed people in them. You might take this idea and do it any number of ways. It is a more creative way to decoupage with photographs than just setting them on a plaque. I'm sure there are other less zany ways to present a family picture, but this should give you the idea. A collage of people and their interests cut from magazines and arranged on a plaque might be another personalized photo collage.

Christmas
Ornaments

Each year I like to think up a new idea for a Christmas card that is decoupaged. One year I made tree ornaments of wood. Each "tree ornament card" was a 1" square, ¼" thick, and had a hole drilled through the top. A gold string was tied through the hole so that the "card" could be tied on the tree. They are fun to make and don't take too much time.

Buy a long strip of wood molding that is about one inch in width. This is sold in wood panel stores, hardware stores, and lumberyards. If the lumberyard will co-operate, have them cut your molding into one inch pieces. If you have a saw and are handy, you can do it yourself. This is really better in the long run because you can paint the entire strip at once, sand it, paint again, and then cut it up —much easier than painting one piece at a time. Sand the pieces on both sides and the edges so that they are smooth. Paint them all white. I used a book for my cutouts, but if you can find some nice Christmas wrapping paper with holly and berries, that would be great. Cut out little red berries and green leaves and design each square very simply with one small decoration in the center or coming down from one corner.

Since the "cards" are so tiny, only a small cutout is required, and you can make many. Using a hand drill, make a small hole in the top of each piece of wood to hold a gold string, the type used for Christmas ornaments. If you can't find the gold string, use red or green velvet ribbon.

When painting and varnishing these wooden pieces line them up on a tray or heavy piece of cardboard so that even though you do them individually, you do them all at the same time. Then when they are all done you can set the entire tray out of the way to dry. When varnishing apply a thin coat so that it won't drip down the sides, making the pieces stick to the tray when dry.

Design the front side only. On the back you will write your greeting. Using an India ink pen, or a pen that will not smear under varnish, write "Merry Christmas from the Smiths" or as I did, "Greetings from Leslie Linsley" or whatever will convey your message in the space. Paint the back of the wooden pieces and sand smoothly before applying your written message. Your writing must be done after painting but before varnishing.

When the ink dries apply a coat or two of varnish to the back and sides so that the paint won't chip or get dirty. Buy enough small envelopes for each of your cards, address them before inserting your wood card, and you have a card that can hang on a tree in each recipient's home.

I did this about four years ago, and I still find my cards hanging on a bulletin board in someone's office. These cards can also be used as a key chain holder after Christmas. It is a continuous reminder of your thoughtfulness. There are always people you want to remember a bit more than a card conveys, and I consider these "cards" between a card and a gift.

You can make these for other occassions as well. There is always scrap wood at lumberyards and mills. Another idea is to buy different sizes of wood chips and make cards of different sizes and designs. In this way each card is custom designed.

You may want to decoupage a photograph of your family on a piece of wood and add a few cutout touches around the photo. This could be a different slant on the photograph Christmas cards many people send. If you use large pieces of wood, such as four or five inches, it might be nice to glue a piece of felt to the back of each. If you insert a brass ring in the top, it can even be hung as a plaque.

This Christmas I decided to send something a little bit different. Instead of using wood I found large plastic clips. They are intended for use as paper holders or as bookmarks and have a hole for hanging. They are great on a bulletin board, and I use them in my studio to hold messages. In the kitchen they are terrific to hold a recipe while you are cooking. I bought several in bright green and cherry red. From one of my books that I had hoarded away I found some unusual plants that looked like red and green berries. I cut sprigs for each clip.

My first surprise was that the glue held the designs to the plastic. My second surprise was that the varnish took to the plastic. I thought! I used a shiny glossy varnish for the clips because the plastic was shiny, and I liked that look for the contemporary objects. The matte is good on wood because of the fine patina of wood, but not for plastic. After three or four coats of varnish I sanded each clip. Rather I started to sand. The varnish began to peel right off. It lifted in the

Christmas card ornaments are made from giant plastic paper clips.

exact way nail polish peels off when you get one part going. Just like lifting skin off chocolate pudding. Well I stopped sanding, FAST. Now here I was with thirty or so clips all cut, designed, and partially varnished. No sanding. That was my solution.

What I did was thin the varnish with a few teaspoonsful of solvent and mixed up the whole thing. This cuts down on the bumps and bubbles. When thinning the varnish it does just that—thins it—but it also eliminates a lot of air bubbles. By doing this you don't have to sand as much. Since I didn't want to sand at all, I needed a lot of help. These clips can't even be breathed upon let alone sanded. When I had applied a few more coats I used a super-fine ⚹0000 steel wool and very, very carefully went over the surface to smooth out any imperfections. These clips do not have the most perfectly smooth surface, but they look real cute and they make a nice Christmas card greeting. Since I couldn't write on the plastic back, I used a small white sticker, placed it on the back, and signed my name on that.

There are many things that you can use for Christmas card-gift giving. Look around in the five and ten for small items.

But not the kitchen sink

As you can see there is almost nothing that you can't decoupage. While you can't decoupage the kitchen sink, you can decoupage the kitchen cabinets. One rainy morning a few summers ago I got into a decorating mood. I had previously painted the cabinets black because they looked so

Decoupaged cabinet door.

dreadful the way they were. I know you can't imagine anything being more dreadful than black for kitchen cabinets, but as I've said before, what's right for one person isn't right for another.

Well now the black cabinets are decorated with large yellow flowers that were cut from a wild flower book. A few coats of varnish to cover and protect, and the project was complete. Everyone tells me they look terrific, but if you are planning to do this don't rush into it. You'll be looking at them forever. It really is a good idea, especially if the cabinets are made of wood and not too exciting. Wallpaper can be used here, and you might pick up the design to use as a border to match your walls.

Many wallpaper designs come in just a border design and this can be very lovely when applied to the bottom half of the doors leaving the top as is. Cut the border out on the top and leave a straight edge on the bottom to line up across the bottom edge of each cabinet door. You will have a running design across or around your room. If you use wallpaper, you can order the exact amount you need. Apply it just as you would put wallpaper on the walls with either wallpaper paste or Elmer's or Sobo. Roll it out well or you will be sure to have lumps. Start in the center at the top of your design and roll outward from the middle to one side and then the next. Wipe the excess glue away as you go. Then varnish over all. If you don't want such a dominating design, use small prints for a narrow border that you create to go around the trim. Or you can simply place one sprig of a flower around each knob. There are a lot of possibilities here.

But, no, you really can't decoupage the kitchen sink.

A wallpaper project

I usually don't encourage the use of wallpaper as a material for decoupage designs. Wallpaper is excellent for lining boxes, but it is not good for the cutout designs for many reasons. First of all, it is too thick to be coated easily with varnish. Also, the paper is often very porous and soaks up the varnish like a sponge. Because of the quality of the paper it is often difficult to do any fine cutting without the outline looking quite choppy. I have also found that some

Planning the design.

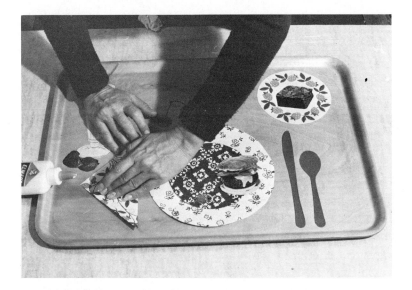

Gluing design in place.

Several coats of varnish finish the tray.

wallpaper discolors in uneven degrees under the varnish. Sometimes the varnish will yellow a white background in spots, leaving other areas unspoiled.

There are, however, other uses for a wallpaper design, and I thought it might be fun to show a different kind of decoupage project using different wallpaper samples. I collect used wallpaper sample books so that I have a constant variety of small pieces to choose from when lining my boxes. These pieces are the perfect size to experiment with. They are often available from the local paint and wallpaper stores. When papers are discontinued the books are thrown out. You can often reserve them for such time.

This project is done on a natural color wood tray. The colors of the wallpaper are red, white, and blue. I decided to make a place setting using contrasting but compatible wallpaper prints. The prints are all rather small and are overall designs. The silverware is cut from red construction paper. I first made an outline around actual silverware and then cut it out. Once the place setting was cut out and planned, it looked a bit plain not to have some food on the plate. I wanted to give the tray a young feeling and searched the magazines for just the right food. The cherries are from a brochure. Usually, it is best to get everything from one source, but this was to be an experiment with papers that I would not ordinarily recommend because of the problems mentioned earlier. As it turned out, the print showed through when varnishing the soda, but faded enough when dry to be acceptable.

While the magazine cutouts were completely submerged after five coats of varnish, it took another five to sufficiently coat the wallpaper cutouts. Therefore, when you run your hand over this tray there are varying degrees of smoothness to the surface. The tray can be used and sponged off for cleaning. I hang it on the wall when not in use.

Teaching decoupage

Teaching decoupage is easy and can be lots of fun whether you are working in a regular school situation or with a craft class. In either case, the best advice I can give is to keep the projects simple. If you start with a small project, there will be less confusion and everyone will be able to finish an item. Most people want to see results right away whether they are ten years old or twenty.

A plaque is usually a good project to begin with, but particularly with kids I like to give them something to make that they can also use. If they all find an interesting container, such as a trinket box for rings, it makes it more fun. They have been doing craft projects with cans since they were in kindergarten, so that's just too uninteresting. The Sucrets tins are a good size as well as Band-aid boxes and bobby pin holders from the five and ten.

Staining is easier than painting, but takes longer to dry. If you buy your supplies—paint, stain, varnish—in large cans, you can divide them up in small quantities using baby jars or something similar that the kids bring in. Cards, magazines, wrapping paper are all useful here as design sources, and everyone can pick what he or she likes best. Always use water-base paint such as acrylic and have cups of clean water handy for cleaning brushes. Poster paint is too thin and will not cover sufficiently. It is best to start out by buying a large quantity of white for everyone for the first project. After this you can mix your own colors using the white for the base. If you get into having everyone choose colors, it will cost a lot more and take up too much class time. I also do not recommend an oil-base varnish for these projects. Use only a polymer medium which you buy in an art supply store. The kids usually like a glossy finish, and this comes in matte or glossy. When applied it looks murky white but dries to a clear finish in less than seven minutes. Some of the brand names for this product are Liquitex, Palmer, Weber, or Grumbacher polymer medium, and it is primarily used for preserving paintings.

The following is a good plan to get you started for the first two classes. The project should be sanded, then painted or stained. While this is drying the students can be cutting out their designs. During the cutting time they should check their item to see if the paint is dry. If so, they should turn from cutting to lightly sanding and applying a second coat of paint.

When the designs are completely cut out (each child will work at his or her own pace) they are ready for gluing. If

the class time is only a half hour, they will barely get the projects painted and sanded and the cutting started. If the class time is an hour, some of the youngsters will begin to glue their designs to the objects.

The second class should be devoted to further cutting and arranging the cutouts in place. Be sure to have plenty of scissors on hand and a safety-edge razor. The latter is used to slit the design where it overlaps from top to bottom if someone is working on a box.

It is a good idea to have some simple finished projects to use as examples of what can be done. While most kids have their own ideas, there will always be a few who really don't have any idea about a design and need some suggestions they can see. Describing doesn't help to visualize. It must be seen.

By the end of the second class everyone should be applying their finish. Usually, by the time the designs are glued in place the students feel they are done—and are ready to go onto the next project. If they have applied a finish, more coats can be applied at the beginning of following classes before they begin to work on new projects.

Encourage them to find objects to bring in and decoupage and tell them to hang onto birthday cards and any other personal items of interest that could be used

If you will be teaching a class of adults, you begin the same way. A small project should be finished by the second class so that your students will be familiar with all the steps involved.

I find a group of six is the most workable, and I think two hours is the ideal length for each class. Usually a group of lessons consists of four or six classes. You should be able to cover all the processes in four classes, but six will give everyone more time to complete two projects.

You will be talking and working with your students while they are painting, cutting, and designing their projects, but the varnishing should be done as homework. I really hate that word "homework," but if they do the varnishing there, they will not be carrying sticky boxes home and you can move on to more meaningful projects sooner. So, sand, paint, and cut for the first hour and a half. During this time describe the process briefly. There is no need to spend the entire time telling about each step in detail since they will be learning in detail as they do each step. During the last half hour everyone will be gluing. This can only be achieved if the projects are small and do not take much designing or cutting of intricate patterns. Avoid this. It is only discouraging. A small trinket box designed with mushrooms is an excellent first project.

By the second class everyone should come back with at least four, if not five coats of varnish on their small item. Remind them not to sand the last coat of varnish so that they will be ready to antique. If anyone has sanded a piece, when returning for the second class, he or she cannot antique this. These students can only watch and either do it on their own or varnish once again and bring it back the following week. Take the time to explain exactly what and why the antiquing is applied. Be sure to have a sample that you can demonstrate on. You will find some may not want to do this. After everyone has antiqued there will be time left to use for discussing questions or problems that each person may have. This may also be done at the beginning of the class, saving the antiquing for last. After working on their items all week your students may have a lot that they are interested in discussing, so it may be better to hold off on your demonstration.

The rest of the first project can be finished on the students own. It is now time to get on with a project that will be designed more carefully. By this time your people should have been looking around for ideas and may already have prints that they are anxious to have you help them with. Talk about choosing designs that will go on their object. Discuss the cutting and warn them against choosing something that is too difficult for them to cut. If possible, try to have them make a box for a second project so that they can learn to line it.

Between the second and third class they should decide what project they will be working on next. If you are teaching in a craft shop where supplies are available, save the last twenty minutes to help the students choose the print and object that they want to work on. If you are limiting each group of lessons to four, they should take the boxes home and do their painting and cutting in preparation for the following week's lesson. If your group of lessons will be six, then they can do their painting and cutting during the following lesson. I find four is comfortable because you don't really need three lessons to learn to paint.

The third class on designing a project is your most important. All the students should be working on their individual projects and should be encouraged to take their time designing. The first time they lay the prints on the box they should take them off and try a second arrangement. You should take time to work with each student for a couple of minutes to help them with their design. Make suggestions, but never impose your design ideas on another. Remember, each person sees it differently.

Try to impress upon them the importance and fun of trying it different ways even if the original arrangment was the best. It's sort of like trying on a dress. If the first one is just right, you aren't as positive and confident about it until you've tried five more. You may go back and buy the first one, but it sure is reassuring when you do.

The last class is devoted primarily to lining a box. Even if they have worked on plaques, it is good to know how to line a box. Have wallpaper samples ready to measure, cut out, and glue into a box as well as some fabric to make another lined with fabric. Some people will be ready to do this; others will just be gluing their designs to their box and will finish on their own unless, of course, you are holding more classes.

Have paste wax available so that everyone who has finished an item will be able to top it off with the final step.

There is no end

I hope some of my projects have inspired you to learn more about decoupage. What's left is what you will add. I can't say that you won't make mistakes, but it's important to know that imperfections add to the handmade quality that is the very nature and charm of a craft.

Each time you do a project you will improve your technical skills as well as your design abilities. Start slowly so that you will be sure to finish each project.

The rewards of making something by hand are far greater than any I can think of. It isn't only the immediate doing that counts, but the lasting value. I think you'll find that the involvement with a craft will make you grow as a person.